The Last Green

Lane Walker

LOCAL LEGENDS
www.bakkenbooks.com

The Last Green by Lane Walker
Copyright © 2023 Lane Walker

Cover Design: Roger Betka

All rights reserved. This book is protected under the copyright laws of the United States of America. This book may not be copied or reprinted for commercial gain or profit.

ISBN 978-1-955657-54-9
For Worldwide Distribution
Printed in the U.S.A.

Published by Bakken Books
2023
www.bakkenbooks.com

*This book is dedicated to
Uncle Rich "Pro" and Aunt Nancy Kitchen.
Thanks for always exemplifying the importance
of family and "hitting the ball straight"
in life and business.*

Local Legends
The Buzzer Beater
The High Cheese
The Storm Blitz
The Last Green

Hometown Hunters Collection
Legend of the Ghost Buck
The Hunt for Scarface
Terror on Deadwood Lake
The Boss on Redemption Road
The Day It Rained Ducks
The Lost Deer Camp

The Fishing Chronicles
Monster of Farallon Islands
The River King
The Ice Queen
The Bass Factory
The Search for Big Lou

For more books, visit: **www.bakkenbooks.com**

-1-

Prologue

The 17th hole on the Pete Dye Stadium course at PGA West in La Quinta is called *Alcatraz*.

Named after the infamous prison of Alcatraz Island located off the San Francisco coast, the island green is considered the toughest hole on the course. The 166-yard par 3 is one of the most challenging holes in entire state of California.

The backdrop of the 17th green was like a Claude Monet painting. The Santa Rosa Mountains tower over the Coachella Valley, giving the landscape a surreal view.

I stood on the tee box, looking straight ahead, and trying to keep my focus on the green. Staying focused was hard as all around me were dangerous hazards. The small island green left little room for error.

"Straight is good; if you're going to miss it, miss it straight," kept running through my mind. I glanced over my right shoulder and made eye contact with Pro.

The look my athletic, confident mentor gave me calmed my racing mind. As soon as we made eye contact, I suddenly knew how he thought I should play this hole.

In the game of golf, the person hits a small white ball off a tee with the goal of getting the ball in the hole with the fewest number of strokes as possible. If that objective alone doesn't sound hard enough, a golf course also features undetected hazards and difficulties. Add in the basics like grip, tempo, and consistency, and the game becomes even harder.

Millions of little, seemingly insignificant aspects can go wrong on the golf course. One small movement or one wrong hand placement can bring complete disaster on the course.

The Last Green

I believe those challenges are what drew me to the game. In addition to the technical and physical demands, the mental side of golf is by far the most intimidating.

I glanced back at Pro.

His stern, focused stare was now fixated on the green. Pro's low voice kept echoing in my head, "Avoid danger; keep your ball straight." Over the past couple of weeks, I thought of the many lessons I had learned from Pro that extended well beyond the fairways and greens of a golf course.

I slowly drew in one last deep breath as I stared toward the 17th hole. As I approached the tee, I tried to block out all the hazards around the hole in the island of green surrounded by water and jagged rocks. This hole had no fairway.

This swing is all or nothing. I knew I had to land my ball on the green if I wanted to take the lead.

My mind raced with all the events over the past month that had brought me this day. I was seemingly destined to play in the championship round of the Best of the West Tournament.

Playing so well the day before had gotten me into the championship round and a pairing with Brady Matthew, the #1 ranked junior golfer.

The small crowd began to grow as word had spread about the final two battling it out for the championship crown. The fact that I was massive underdog in the tournament didn't hurt the storyline. Some familiar faces were in the crowd, but most were strangers.

My mind started to race with doubt. "Stop!" I told myself. "Not this time!" I took control of my mind, focusing only on my tee shot.

I stood in the tee box, trying not to notice the jagged, crooked rocks or the towering mountains in the background. My vision narrowed as I watched the small blue flag blowing lightly in the wind.

Alcatraz was in front of me.

"Miss straight, miss straight," I whispered to myself as I took my backswing.

I was down one shot…with two holes to go.

This is my chance.

-2-

I love living in the Palm Springs area. My home is actually in La Quinta, which is about 25 minutes from Palm Springs. Commonly referred to as the golf capital of the world, Palm Springs is located on the western edge of the Colorado Desert in Southern California.

When most people think of California, they think of beaches, movie stars and the Pacific Ocean, which doesn't properly describe Palm Springs. This inland city is close enough to Los Angeles and San Diego to attract locals as well as many out-of-state visitors.

What is the main attraction to Palm Springs? Golf! Over 150 golf courses spread over the Palm

Springs area, and the weather is perfect for hitting the links.

Palm Springs is also recognized for the list of celebrities who vacation there. The city started to gain notoriety in the 1920s as Hollywood movie stars took the two-hour drive east from Los Angeles. A-list stars bought second homes in Palm Springs that became their oasis retreat from the busy city life.

Once this "paradise" was discovered, the Palm Springs' population exploded as stars like Frank Sinatra; Dean Martin; Sammy Davis, Jr.; Bob Hope; Elvis Presley; Marilyn Monroe; Dinah Shore; Lucille Ball; and Elizabeth Taylor fell in love with the area. Shortly thereafter, American Presidents including Dwight Eisenhower, John F. Kennedy, Ronald Reagan, and Barack Obama became frequent visitors. After the Roaring 20s and throughout history, more star-studded names flocked to Palm Springs. Modern-day stars like Leonardo DiCaprio, Brad Pitt, and the Kardashians vacation in this glamorous getaway.

The Last Green

I wasn't impressed with all the movie stars... Instead, I found all the professional golfers who visited Palm Springs more amazing than any of the Hollywood people. Seemingly, a pro was always playing in Palm Springs or attending one of the huge golf tournaments. For a kid who loved golf, seeing a pro was way more impressive than any movie or rock star!

My family took a lot of pride in Palm Springs and its surrounding area. My grandpa had moved our family to Palm Springs from Chicago when my dad was two years old.

Grandpa Ron, who everyone called Pops, was in the construction business, and for that line of work, there was no better place than Palm Springs. New construction in the Coachella Valley was expanding at a rapid rate. Work was easy to find, and eventually Grandpa started his own construction business designing and building golf courses. Taylor Builders had an excellent reputation and was now managed by my dad.

Dad worked frequently in the valley, but he

also traveled the world building elite golf courses. Due to my family's business and passion for golf I fell in love with the sport at a young age. When I was younger, Dad would frequently take me to the land before building a new course. I loved seeing a bare spot of desert and imagining what the course would look like. My favorite part was returning after its completion, to see his vision become reality, and then playing the course that Dad had helped build.

Dad had many connections in the golf world. When I was six years old, we started golfing together so that I could learn the game from him. Now at age 14, I was known around the valley as one of the best junior golfers in the area.

I had already played more rounds of golf than most adults, typically playing five to six rounds a week. Dad was always my favorite playing partner and helped me as well. He was a good golfer and taught me everything he could.

I had grown up playing in some of the smaller youth and junior golf tournaments around Palm

Springs. I had even won several of the tournaments, and my name was now being mentioned as an up-and-coming golfer.

Everything was going well, and I was playing fantastic golf heading into the Spring Showcase Tournament at the Indian Wells Country Club.

I was up six strokes heading into the third and final day of the tournament. All I had to do was stay focused and play consistent golf.

If only the game were that easy...

-3-

A large crowd started to gather as I rounded the 12th hole. My lead had fallen to three strokes as I bogeyed holes #1, #4 and #6. A *bogey* is when a golfer scores one stroke over par on any hole. *Par* is a set score in strokes for each hole. That score indicates how many strokes it should take a golfer to get the ball in the hole. If a hole is labeled a par four, a golfer should get the golf ball in the cup in four hits.

I was able to par the other holes, but I surely wasn't playing my best golf. I kept glancing at the leaderboard as my nerves started to get the best of me.

The game of golf has a way of exposing each

player's weaknesses. The best golfers are able to perfect these weak aspects of their game to limit or eliminate mistakes.

For me, I was pretty good with the mechanics of hitting my clubs. *Putting* is probably my greatest strength followed by my irons. I also spent a lot of time at the driving range this past summer, which had greatly improved my swing off the tee.

I hit bad shots like every golfer, but my iron game was elite for someone my age. My biggest hurdle to overcome was my lack of confidence, which was magnified when large groups of people watched me. The mental side of golf remained a huge challenge for me.

Only two things in life really scared me. The first was heights, and the second was golfing in front of a crowd of people. My dad tried and tried to help me develop a strong will and confidence, but something always changed when a crowd showed up. Only four or five spectators didn't really bother me. I had studied and watched enough golf to know that if I couldn't master the mental side of the game, I wouldn't be able to win at a high level, no matter how much I improved my mechanics.

My hands started to sweat as I gripped my club. I approached my ball and took a practice swing. *It doesn't feel right!* I knew my grip was too tight as I tensed up through my swing. I took a deep breath and backed off the tee.

My mind started racing with negative thoughts. *You're going to shank it. Everyone is watching you. You're going to fail.*

I glanced back toward my dad who shot a stern look back at me.

I don't want to let him down.

He could tell what was happening to me. He had grown frustrated with my negative self-talk. He had spent many hours talking to me about blocking my negative thoughts and believing in myself. I couldn't explain or prepare for these counteractive thoughts.

I didn't know how to avoid them. Something within me triggered the expectation of the worst.

I took another deep breath and lined up my

driver. I told myself, "Colt, you got this; you've hit this shot a thousand times."

After several seconds of nervous anticipation, I brought my club back and swung. I knew in the middle of my back swing that something bad was going to happen. I tried to correct my swing and ended up taking my eye off the ball. As I swung through, the face of my driver clipped the inside of the ball.

The drive was disastrous as it skipped down the fairway and landed 30 yards from the tee box. When a low sigh passed through the crowd, I knew that I had let my nerves win once again. I didn't look in my dad's direction. I slammed my driver against my golf bag in anger.

I was hitting two and still had almost four hundred yards to the green. I knew I was in big trouble and had completely lost all confidence on the hole. I badly mishit the next shot and then sliced the following one. The 12th hole was a disaster.

I ended up shooting a nine on the hole and lost the lead. The rest of the round wasn't much better.

When I finally putted out on the 18th hole, I was in tenth place. I went from first place to tenth in the last six holes of the tournament. Instead of holding the giant trophy and getting my picture taken for the newspaper, I had the lonely walk of shame to the clubhouse.

The other golfers avoided me and gave me a I-feel-sorry-for-you look as I passed them. I had planned on attending the dinner after the championship. I could smell the food as I entered the clubhouse. I handed my official scorecard to the attendant behind the table. Instead of going into the banquet room, I walked back out and grabbed my golf bag.

My dad was walking toward me, and he could tell by the expression of my face that dinner was not going to happen.

"Take a deep breath, Colt. Having some bad holes is part of the game. I know it hurts, son, but that's the game of golf," he calmly stated.

I tried to talk but was struggling with emotions. I knew I was on the verge of tears.

"Okay, Dad. Let's just go," I finally muttered.

He nodded.

I was upset that I had choked badly in the golf tournament. I knew that I had only had myself to blame.

As we walked to the car, I tried to tell myself that this tournament would be the last time I let my nerves control me.

Little did I know this loss would prove to be only the beginning of my problems.

-4-

The 20-minute ride home was silent. I appreciated my dad's giving me some time to myself.

I knew the problem was me and my internal thoughts, which had led to my meltdown. My mind raced with more negative thoughts as we drove. I tried to block them out and replace them with images of all the good shots.

The 25-foot putt on the 16th hole and a near chip in on hole three were both amazing golf shots. Even those great shots couldn't clear my mind; I kept going over my tee shot on the 12th hole.

I finally spoke as Dad reached for the garage door opener. "Dad, could we jump on the golf cart and hit the driving range?"

The Last Green

Our house was located at Mountain View Country Club. Dad and I were both members, and our house bordered the #12 tee box. We had moved there five years ago and loved the location. We tried to play the course at least twice a week, and I tried to hit balls on the driving range as much as I could. Everyone knew us on the course. We spent hours on the back patio and in the swimming pool, observing golfers as they played the 12th hole.

"Not tonight, Colt," he answered. "You haven't seen your mom this entire weekend."

I knew I should stay home, but I really wanted to work on my golf swing.

"Son, I don't think the range is what you need to address. Of course, I think the mechanics are important, but your swing is not what cost you that tournament."

I nodded. *He's right.* As we walked into the house, I felt the comfort of being home. My mom's sweet smile and quick hug put my mind at ease.

"Hey, Colt, Dad texted me updates and told me you did your best," Mom said.

"I got tenth place," I said.

"That's great! Be proud of that accomplishment. You could have gotten eleventh," she said, trying to cheer me up.

Minutes later I heard a loud knock on the front door.

"Come on in, boys," Mom called from the kitchen. She didn't need to look through the peephole, and we all knew who was there by the aggressive sound of the knock.

The front door flung open, and I delightedly greeted Bob and Andy, my next-door neighbors and best friends.

Every day I hung out with Bob and Andy, who were twin brothers. We had become friends as soon as I had moved to Mountain View. Thankfully, both were in my third-grade class, which made the move to a new school much easier.

Since that first day we met, we became almost inseparable, doing everything together. We loved to swim, fish in the ponds around our subdivision, and golf together.

"Did you win? Tell me you won! Where's the trophy?" yelled Bob enthusiastically.

Andy could tell by the look on my face that I hadn't won.

"No biggie if you didn't…I mean that tournament is full of great golfers," Andy said.

"I placed tenth," I said.

"Okay, what happened to your lead?" questioned Bob. I knew Bob wasn't being rude, but I was trying to avoid talking about my meltdown. The night before we had hung out together playing video games, so they knew I was in first place heading into the final day of the tournament.

"I let my mind get the best of me," I finally admitted.

"That's easy to do on the golf course; we all know that. Don't beat yourself up over it," encouraged Andy.

Both Bob and Andy were pretty good golfers, and we played golf almost every day during the summer. As good as they were, I was much better than both. But like true best friends, they were my biggest fans. There was no jealousy; they always supported me.

"You know, you're too good for that to still be happening," Bob said.

"I know, but I just got to figure it out," I said.

"You will," offered Andy.

With that comment, the pair took off for my bedroom. We spent the rest of the night playing video games and eating pizza.

Even though the night had started on a sour note, it ended up being a good one. Eventually the memory of my12th hole meltdown faded, and I was able to enjoy the company of my friends.

-5-

Sunday mornings were always special.

Bob, Andy, Dad, and I pretty much always played 18 holes of golf before church. We had started this tradition three years ago, and we always had a blast.

Because of our frequent visits to the golf course, the employees at Mountain Valley knew us all by name and treated us well.

The morning was going great, and our group was playing well on the front nine. I held a slim one-shot lead over my dad; Bob and Andy were both four over. I was getting to a point in my golf game where I was regularly beating Dad, who was a great golfer. He definitely wasn't the kind of father who would simply let his kid always win either.

At the *turn*, the break between holes 9 and 10 at the clubhouse, we stopped in the pro shop to grab water and a granola bar. Bob and Andy went in to use the restroom as I stood staring out the window at the greens full of familiar golfers.

Suddenly, I noticed someone new on the course. Having lived there and played the course so often, I knew most of the people, but I had never seen this tall, athletic man. I was shocked to see him playing by himself and walking. Most of the time, we used a golf cart. Sometimes when Dad and I were bored at night, we would walk and shoot a couple holes. But anytime we played 18 holes, we rented a cart.

Something about this guy drew my attention. His walk was smooth and his stride sure as he finished the 9th hole and walked toward the tenth.

I had no problem with letting him play through our game. I knew if we didn't, this single golfer would be waiting behind us on the entire back nine.

I was still studying the new guy as Bob and Andy walked up.

"Who's that?" asked Bob.

"I'm not sure," I answered.

The three of us watched as he hit his drive off the tenth tee box. We stared in awe as he crushed his ball—straight as an arrow down the fairway.

By the time the ball bounced in the middle of the fairway, he was in pursuit. His driver was already back in his bag, and he was walking toward his ball.

"Man, that guy can golf!" exclaimed Andy. "His form is perfect."

"Yeah, so smooth," I replied as I took off for the exit toward our cart. I wanted to watch his second shot. I stepped up on the side of the golf course so I could get a better view. The golfer approached his ball, took one practice swing, and hit his iron.

I watched in amazement as the ball took two big hops and stopped short mere inches from the hole.

"That guy almost holed out from 190 yards!" Bob exclaimed.

His swing was once again flawless—just like his tee shot.

I squinted as the golfer walked over and picked up his ball without even putting. His golf ball sat so close to the hole he must have figured he was close enough. From our viewpoint, the ball appeared to be sitting on the edge of the hole, but in reality, it was probably a few inches from the cup.

Something stirred inside me. *I have to see more!* I jumped in the cart and took off down the 10th fairway.

I heard someone yell and glanced back to see my dad standing there after returning from the pro shop.

"I'll be right back," I yelled.

Both Bob and Andy sat on their cart puzzled. They didn't try to follow me. I was on a mission; I wanted to see this guy tee off on the 11th hole.

I knew the next hole was a 187-yard par three.

I crested the hill right in time to see his white ball hit the back of the green and slowly roll back. Once again, he was less than a foot from the hole!

Every shot he took was perfectly straight and looked like something off the Golf Channel.

I had seen many amazing golfers in my short life on the golf course, but I had never seen someone with such a fluid swing. *Something is really special about this golfer.*

I turned back to see my dad waving me back to the 10th tee box. I figured I had better return so we didn't slow down the group approaching behind us. I pushed the pedal on the golf cart and circled back toward the clubhouse.

When I got halfway up the fairway, I turned back. I wanted to get the man's name or see where he was from.

He's gone! He had disappeared like a ghost.

As I drove back to the tee box to rejoin my group, I started to second-guess myself.

Was he ever even there?

-6-

"Son, what on earth are you doing?" Dad asked. He looked confused as I pulled toward the tee box. "I saw this guy…and his swing…" I started to explain.

"We don't have time for that right now, Colt," Dad interrupted. "I didn't see anyone in front of us. Two foursomes just went into the clubhouse. They will be breathing down our necks if we don't hit," he said.

I glanced toward Bob and Andy. Their heads were down, so I knew they weren't going to help me by telling Dad they had also seen the golfer.

Since I had the lowest score, I teed off first. I looked down the long par 4 fairway. In my mind, the mystery golfer's booming drive kept replaying in my mind.

I couldn't break my stare.

"Any day now, son," Dad quietly whispered. He liked to play at a perky pace and was starting to get antsy as we were delaying the group behind us.

I drew back and without hesitating or thinking crushed a perfectly straight drive down the center of the fairway. The shot floated through the air and landed hard in the middle of the fairway, rolling another 20 to 30 yards.

"Wow! Now that's what I'm talking about," said Bob.

"I don't want to have to tee off next after that shot," joked Andy.

Dad grinned. I knew he was proud of me and how hard I had worked to become a good golfer. The drive was my best of the day so far. The only thing I thought about during my backswing was the crisp, smooth swing of the mystery man.

I wanted my swing to be fluid and flawless like his. On that swing, it was. I played well the rest of the round and ended up shooting 2 under par. My dad shot 1 over par, while Bob and Andy, both good golfers, shot 4 over.

After we putted out the 18th hole, I shot a glance toward the clubhouse.

"Dad, I will run in the cart keys," I volunteered quickly.

He nodded and grabbed both of our club bags, and started walking toward his SUV. Andy and Bob followed as I walked into the pro shop.

"Thanks, Colt," said Tony, who was standing behind the counter.

He added, "How was your round?"

"Not bad. I ended up beating my dad so that makes me happy," I said with a chuckle.

"You got that right," he said. Tony Lamont, the club pro, was in his mid-twenties and was working toward earning his professional tour card. I had heard a lot about his skill level and how good his golf game was.

He had attended the University of Arizona on a golf scholarship and was first team all-conference his senior year. His game was solid, and his life revolved around the game of golf.

"Tony, who was the guy golfing in front of us?" I asked.

"The guy? I think you had a foursome in front of you. But don't quote me, let me check," he said walking over to the reservation book that held all the tee times.

He looked confused as he scanned the text.

"Looks like Doc Murphy's foursome was in front of you—at least that's who was in the book this morning," he answered.

I knew Doc Murphy, so I knew it wasn't him, and one man definitely wasn't a foursome.

"Nah, it was only one guy," I said.

"One guy?" he said, puzzled. He was thinking what I was; it's uncommon for a single golfer to be on the course in the morning.

"Why are you so interested in this guy?" Tony asked.

"Something about him and the way he hit the golf ball was different," I said.

"Sounds like a guy I would like to hit the links with," Tony considered.

I could tell Tony had no idea who the mystery man was. I thanked him and waved as I left.

I had no doubt that I had seen an exceptional golfer. I knew Bob and Andy had seen him. His swing kept replaying over and over in my mind.

I knew I had to find this guy because one thing was obvious to me: whoever this mystery man was, he had to be my next golf instructor.

I want to learn to swing like him.

-7-

Having someone new on the course wasn't uncommon. I found it interesting though that I had never seen this golfer before.

What's more, this guy was obviously an elite golfer. In the golfing community, elite golfers, the ones who are on the top of the game, are talked about around Palm Springs like celebrities.

We headed home to get ready for church. We all attended the same church located only a couple miles from our house. My encounter with the stranger on the golf course had almost made us late for church!

Fortunately, our family walked in right on time. Halfway through the service, I noticed Bob and

Andy's family had also made it as they sat closer to the back.

When church ended, I was excited to get home and spend some time with the guys in our pool. I quickly changed and jumped in the pool, waiting for Bob and Andy to join me. After a couple minutes, both boys cannonballed into the pool.

"Thanks for helping me out earlier with my dad," I commented sarcastically.

"Your dad wouldn't care about some long golfer. You know how important it is to golf at a good pace," said Andy.

Our conversation was interrupted when Bob flew off the edge of the pool and cannonballed almost on top of me. The wave knocked me under water, and I popped up gasping for air.

I looked at Bob who was already staring at me.

The three of us burst out laughing and started splashing each other. Something is special about hanging out with your best friend, or in my case, best *friends*. Bob and Andy were like brothers to me; they had a way of making me laugh like no one else could. I always had friends with whom to toss the football, play video games, and go golfing. We owned the summers and had a blast spending time together.

As the three of us teased each other and wrestled in the pool. Dad came out and started the grill to cook his famous chicken kabobs.

As Dad was rotating the chicken, he said, "Hey, there's Tony. It looks like he is about to tee off on the 12th." The three of us scrambled to the side of the pool for a better view. We loved watching good golfers tee off.

Tony stepped up to the tee and hit an iron toward the flag. His ball bounced safely on the green and settled about 25 feet from the pin. The shot was good, and he had a long putt for birdie. We watched as his ball slowly came to stop. We started cheering for Tony. He was too far away to hear us but cheering for him was still fun.

Then something amazing happened.

As we were cheering, another ball flew into our view and landed on this green. Only this ball was much closer and had back spin. Our mouths were hanging open as we watched the tiny white ball come to a stop right next to the flagpole. This shot made Tony's great shot look inferior.

My eyes traced back to the tee box, and my jaw dropped. My mystery man from this morning was picking up his tee and then sliding into the golf cart with Tony.

"That's him," I shrieked, pulling myself out of the pool. I ran toward the lawn chair and grabbed my towel. I could hear Bob and Andy shuffling behind me as I ran through my house toward the front door. I knew that if I hurried, I could catch them crossing the road toward the 13th tee box.

I had to hustle. I knew golfers like that didn't take much time putting. I sprinted toward the crossing as Bob and Andy trailed closely behind me.

I dashed the 200 yards to the crossing only stopping to put my hands on my knees. I looked down the cart path to my left. *Nothing! Did I miss them? Did I manage to lose him once again?*

-8-

Bob and Andy caught up and looked like they were about ready to collapse. Their shoulders were heavy, and they were struggling to catch their breath.

"Where is he?" Andy asked huffing and puffing.

"I don't know! I don't know!" I said frantically.

The three of us stood dripping wet, wrapped in towels. We must have looked like fools galloping down the road toward the crossway.

Seconds felt like minutes as we waited and waited. After about four or five minutes, we heard the low tone of a golf cart. Cresting the hill and coming down the trail to cross to the 13th tee was Tony and the mystery man.

We didn't miss them! I'm finally going to meet this elite golfer!

As they came closer, Tony waved before stopping in front of us.

"Colt? Andy? Bob? What's up, fellas?" he asked, obviously trying to figure out why we were soaking wet and waiting there.

I looked at Tony and gave him a weird look as my eyes shifted from Tony to the other golfer.

Finally, Tony picked up on the hint.

"Oh, boys, let me introduce you to Rich Kitchen," he said.

Rich Kitchen?

Strange, the name didn't strike an immediate chord, but I knew I had heard that name someplace before.

The mystery man, who was in his mid-60s, was in great shape. He sported a visor and a golfer's tan. I could tell he golfed a lot as I could see a small white band of skin under his watch.

"Hello, sir," I finally mustered.

The man politely nodded.

I felt a moment of awkwardness as the five of us exchanged glances. I finally piped up, "Tony, this is the golfer I was telling you about today."

Now the reason why the three of us were standing there wrapped in towels suddenly clicked for Tony. I could tell by his facial expression that he finally understood why we were holding up their golf game.

The man looked confused, but Tony wasn't.

"Colt thinks you're a pretty good golfer," he told Rich and chuckled.

Rich smiled and turned in my direction. "I just love playing the game. I tell myself that I'm in good shape if I miss it straight," he said in a soft tone.

His comment caused all of us to laugh.

"Don't worry, you guys will be seeing more of Rich on the course. Rich and his wife Nancy recently bought a house on Boone Avenue overlooking the 17th hole. Anyway, Pro and I have to go; we need to keep pace on our round," said Tony.

As soon as I heard Boone Avenue, my mind started reeling. *Boone Avenue? The nicest houses on*

Mountain Valley Golf Course were on Boone Avenue! I barely noticed he called the man *Pro* as they were leaving.

The golf cart sputtered, and the two men were off toward the 12th.

"Man, why does it feel like we somehow know that guy?" Andy asked.

"I know what you're saying. There's something about him. For him to live on Boone Avenue, he must have made some major coin. Maybe he owned a franchise or was famous for something. The only people I know on Boone Avenue are on another level, man," Bob added.

Bob was right. Boone Avenue was not only one of the premiere streets in Mountain Valley, but it was also one of the best places in all the Palm Springs area. The stories about Boone Avenue were crazy. My dad had told me when we first moved here that the rumor was Elvis Presley once owned a house on Boone Avenue. I know at least two former professional athletes called Boone Avenue home.

The Last Green

I stood there thinking for a couple seconds.

"It's not Boone Avenue," I said.

"What's not Boone Avenue?" Andy asked.

"Rich...this Rich Kitchen...I'm sure he has money, but something tells me he doesn't care very much about all that," I said.

"How do you know that?" Bob asked.

"I am not sure how to explain it; I just know," I answered.

The weird thing was, I simply sensed that something was special about this Rich Kitchen—this mystery man with an amazing swing. After all, I didn't have any facts or other knowledge.

My intuition was right. As soon as I got home, Dad asked me what was going on. When I told him, he confirmed everything I had been thinking.

Indeed, there was something amazing and special about our new neighbor on Boone Avenue.

-9-

Bob and Andy headed home to have lunch with their family, and I walked back toward the grill.

"What's up, Colt? Why'd you boys take off like that?" Dad asked while scrubbing the grill. He used a big scrubber that was outfitted with black pads. His grill was immaculate, and Dad took great pride in keeping it in mint condition.

"Does the name Rich Kitchen mean anything to you?" I curiously inquired.

Dad stopped and looked toward the sky. I could tell he was deep in thought, trying to access the wide array of names and people that he knew. "No, not offhand," he finally replied. "Why?"

I told Dad the story about the man at the golf

course and our encounter with Tony and Rich. Dad listened intently, leaving his grill duties to focus on our conversation.

"You said he lives on Boone Avenue? He must have done something right in his life..." Dad chuckled.

"But that's not it, Dad. I can tell it's not a money thing. His swing is the best I have ever seen."

"Maybe he's nothing more than a rich guy with a good golf swing," Dad said, going back to scrubbing the grill. "Let the man enjoy Mountain Valley. I'm sure he's getting in a good round with Tony."

I agreed and walked toward the house to change into dry clothes. Just as I was about to enter through the glass sliding doors, Dad yelled, "Now if 'Pro' Kitchen showed up, that might cause me to run like a madman down the street too," he said with a sly smile.

Wait, what did Dad say? Did I hear him right? I stopped in my tracks and turned back toward him.

"What did you say, Dad? I don't think I heard you," I said.

"Well, I was only joking, Son. I said if Pro Kitchen was here, now that would be a big deal!" he said.

"But, Dad, I heard Tony call him *Pro*. I didn't know what he meant though," I said.

"Son, I doubt it," Dad said, shaking his head with a half-smile on his face. "If Pro was here, the entire valley would know."

"Why? Who is Pro Kitchen?" I asked.

"Who is Pro Kitchen? I thought I had taught you a lot about the game of golf," Dad said, pretending to be shocked.

I stood still, fully engaged in our conversation. Dad could tell I wasn't budging or moving until he explained who Pro was.

"Richard 'Pro' Kitchen was born in Grand Rapids, Michigan. During his high school years, he fell in love with golf and his next-door neighbor Nancy. The two became high school sweethearts and soon after got married. They both loved each other and the game of golf, and the game loved them back.

"Pro was an incredible golfer, and his wife Nancy was no slouch either. Instead of going to college, Pro set out to quickly earn his professional tour card. He had a long career playing in mostly smaller tour events. He even played in some of the big ones but never came out on top. His career was long, and most of his wins came at overseas golf tournaments.

"One thing Pro was known for was speaking his mind and standing up for what he believed in.

"I heard that he spoke out against one of the most prestigious golf courses on the PGA tour at the time. Back then, they were very selective of who they allowed to play the course. The rumor was that women and certain ethnic groups weren't allowed to golf there," Dad explained.

"That's horrible! Why wouldn't everyone be allowed to play golf?" I asked.

"The bigotry back then was horrible, and the rules were different. People had unyielding viewpoints, and sadly, they weren't happy with Pro's vocal disagreement with their rules. He refused to play in the event, and his refusal cost him several sponsors. The media even steered clear of him."

Dad continued, "Everyone knew Pro Kitchen was an elite, masterful golfer. He went on to win the Canadian Open, the Australian Open and several smaller events. The good news is, he had a brilliant career and made a great deal of money doing something he loved."

After Dad filled me in, I almost couldn't believe what he had shared with me.

Dad then added, "Last I heard, he was retired and living in Las Vegas, but that was years ago. Anyone who knows anything about golf knows that Pro Kitchen is a golfing legend. Are you're sure that's who you met?"

"Yes, Dad, I am 100 percent sure that our new neighbor is Pro Kitchen."

I knew it—just like I knew something was special about Pro when I had seen him earlier.

I knew what I had to do next, and that one thought kept running through my mind.

I need to convince Pro Kitchen to become my new golf teacher.

-10-

After dinner that night, Bob and Andy came over and with my parents' permission, we researched all about Pro on the Internet.

We found websites with information about him. A fantastic golfer, Pro had competed for a long time and had made a lot of money. He had never won any of the PGA Majors, but Kitchen had a long, healthy, and very profitable golfing career.

The last website we clicked on showed his career money earnings. Even though Pro never won any of the major PGA events, he still managed to make millions during his golfing career. I knew he would have made even more with sponsorships and event signings.

"Well, that information confirms he definitely doesn't need the money to give me lessons," I said.

"Yeah, but fame and fortune doesn't always mean snobby or closed-minded," said Andy.

"I only know one way to find out," I said. "Let's get up early tomorrow and ask Pro if he would consider training me."

"Like you mean, we should go golfing and hope to run into him on the course?" Andy asked.

"No, let's drive our golf cart down and wait for him on the first tee box," I said.

"But we don't know what time he will be there," Bob debated.

"What time did we see him on the 10th hole today?" I asked.

"I would guess it was around 10:00 a.m. or so since we teed off at 8:05 a.m.," said Andy.

"Tomorrow morning, we will be waiting on the first tee at seven o'clock. That should be around the time that Pro golfs," I said.

"Seven o'clock. on a Monday morning? We have school tomorrow," said Andy.

"You guys do what you want; I will be waiting at seven o'clock on the tee box," I said.

"Then we will be there too," Bob declared.

That night I tossed and turned. I was filled with excitement, thinking about the fact that a professional golfer could possibly be my new instructor. *If I could just get a swing like Pro's, then I could overcome my self-doubt and insecurities on the golf course.*

But another thought kept creeping into my mind that wasn't exciting; it was scary. *What if he has no interest in helping me? Am I ready for that type of rejection?*

My mind started to play tricks on me again, and all my confidence was suddenly gone.

Instead of thinking positive thoughts, my mind became filled with negative ones. By the time I finally fell asleep, I was convinced that Pro was going to say no and I would be on my own again.

What do I have to do to convince him? How can I make him see my potential?

I felt sure Tony had told him that I was a really

good golfer—one of the best 12-year-olds in the entire Coachella Valley.

But will that be enough? Will Pro even care?

He had done his time on the golf course and had done well.

Will he be interested in helping some young kid he doesn't even know?

-11-

The grass was moist with morning dew as we sat on the first tee box. Only Andy was with me; Bob was still home in bed. He'd always been a heavy sleeper, and I knew last night that getting him out of bed an hour earlier than usual would take a miracle.

We didn't see any fresh footprints on the tee box, so we knew as of yet no one had teed off.

Ten minutes went by before we heard the humming sound of a golf cart approaching. I recognized Tony from a distance.

"Boys, don't you have school?" he asked when he came closer.

"We do, and we are going. We were hoping to see Pro first," I said.

Tony smiled and leaned back in his cart.

"You got up early to see Pro before school? Wow! You guys must really be star-struck," he said.

I almost told him our reason for being here—that we weren't here hoping for an autograph, but for a chance to see if he could help me with my golf game.

"Pro started on the back nine this morning, so if you plan on seeing him here it might be a while," he said.

"The back nine?" I questioned.

"Yeah, he likes to mix it up, so he is starting on the back of the course today," said Tony.

My mind started to play tricks on me, and all my excitement left my body.

"Okay, thanks," I said motioning toward Andy to sit back.

Without saying another word, I turned the cart and took off toward our house.

"Good, we're going home. I don't want to be late for school," said Andy.

"Not quite," I said.

The Last Green

I knew that our only hope was to catch Pro on the 12th hole—the same place we had seen him yesterday. Luckily, I knew every shortcut and turn on the golf course.

Just as we were crossing the street to 12th, we saw the back of a golf cart in front of us. I zoomed over the hill and spotted Pro walking on the green. I slowed down and parked next to his cart. Pro was on his own, and we watched as he lined up his putt. The ball, which was about 20 feet away from the cup, was in a bad spot. His putt was uphill and had a pretty big break.

Pro wasted no time after squaring up his putt, and smoothly guiding his putter through the ball. We watched in amazement as the ball steadily plowed uphill before breaking hard to the right and dropping into the hole.

"Wow!" Andy whispered.

I was amazed. That was a tough putt, but I knew he would make it.

Pro also *knew* he would make it.

He grabbed his ball and started to walk back to

his golf cart. Suddenly seeing us, he looked surprised, came closer, and asked, "Boys, don't you have school?"

"Yes, sir. We're going to go to school, I promise," I stammered.

"Good to hear because school is very important," he said.

"Nice putt by the way," Andy quickly interjected.

"Thanks, it felt good. I always try to keep it in the short grass," said Pro.

Keep it in the short grass? I thought. *Man, this guy is full of great one liners.* I knew right away what he meant: hit the golf ball straight and stay away from potential hazards and dangers on the golf course. Following his own established ways was one reason why Pro was such a phenomenal golfer.

Andy and I sat there amazed and speechless. It wasn't every day you could learn from a real-life, professional golfer.

After a couple of awkward seconds, Pro finally

spoke. "Is there anything else I can help you boys with?"

I started to respond, but suddenly my throat was tight, and my tongue felt too big for my mouth.

I was nervous. I knew what I wanted to say, but I was struggling to say it. When I finally spoke, I muttered something about wanting to be good at golf that barely sounded like words. I knew I was blowing my shot.

"Pro, is there any way you would work with Colt? He's one of the best junior golfers around. He could be really good if someone like you would help him," Andy said.

I was so thankful I had brought Andy with me. Just like a true friend, Andy had come through for me when I needed him the most.

Pro drew a deep, long breath. "Train Colt?" he said, stroking his chin. He turned to look me square in the eyes.

I was sure my eyes looked like they were begging. I had the same look I gave my mom when we saw our dog, Major, as a puppy at the pet shop.

Begging eyes are hard to say no to, I thought.

After a couple of long seconds, Pro spoke. "I don't think you want me to be your coach. The last time I trained a young up-and-comer didn't end well."

My heart dropped in pure disappointment.

See you're not that good. He doesn't want to waste his time training some average golfer from La Quinta.

Pro turned and hopped in his cart. The two of us just sat there, feeling dejected. Andy felt bad for me.

Pro's cart started and took off. He drove for a few seconds before coming to a screeching halt.

He turned and called something in our direction that Andy and I had to strain to hear. "Be here after school. We can play some golf," he yelled.

"Hey, at least he didn't say no!" Andy said hopefully.

"Yeah, but that still doesn't mean he wants to be my coach," I said.

-12-

Andy and I got back just in time to jump in the car and catch a ride with my mom on her way to work. Bob staggered out of their house, dragging his feet, still half asleep as usual.

"What happened, guys? What did I miss?" he asked, wiping the sleep from his eyes.

"Oh, we're going golfing after school," I said.

"Okay. We golf almost every day after school," Bob said.

"Today, we're golfing with Pro," Andy said from the seat behind us.

This reply perked up Bob, and his eyes quickly widened.

"Really? That's awesome! I have always wanted

to golf with a professional," Bob said. "I'm going to text Mom to iron my funky Hawaiian golf shirt!"

"Me too," Andy said excitedly.

I smiled, but I wasn't as excited as I should be. My fear of failure was now stopping me from enjoying a great opportunity.

I was nervous, and questions haunted me. *Would I play well with Pro watching? If this is my one chance to impress him, will I? Will this simply be another chance for me to choke and let everyone down again, including myself?*

That school day passed as one of the fastest I can remember. School days usually dragged on, seeming to last forever, but not today. There was nothing I could do to slow the day down.

By the time lunchtime came around, Bob and Andy had already told practically everyone about our big chance to golf with Pro. The guys at our lunch table started asking me a bunch of questions. I smiled and acted like I had the best opportunity in the world.

Then Nate Jeffery asked the question that had

been burning in my mind all day: "Man, I don't think I would like to play with a professional golfer. Won't it be hard for someone like that to golf with you guys?" he asked.

Bobby Evans piped up from the back of our table. "Colt is one of the best golfers I have ever seen," he said.

Bob and Andy turned and looked at me with a scared look on their face.

I could tell Nate's question was the first time the thought of playing with Pro and not doing well had even crossed their minds.

"I'm not worried about Colt, but now I am a little worried about myself. I mean I'm a good golfer—but certainly not great," Bob said.

Andy nodded in agreement.

"You got nothing to worry about; you're way better than both of us," Bob said as he patted me on the back.

Suddenly, I was terrified to play badly in front of Pro.

How could we even think we could play a round

of golf with someone at his level? Will I disappoint him and waste his time?

I knew I had to play an incredible round of golf if I had any chance of convincing him to take me on as his student.

As I got up from the lunch table to throw my plate away, my stomach started hurting. The fear of failing was digging deeper roots in my mind…and now in my body too.

The rest of the day I tried to think positive thoughts. I had played Mountain Valley hundreds of times and usually shot well. I was the Junior Club Champion and held the course record for kids 14 and under. However, a new shadow of a doubt was now starting to form that was finding a way to crack my entire confidence.

My stomach continued to ache for the rest of the day. I was thankful that I had only one hour of school left, my last class for the day. I also knew this meant I was one hour away from golfing with Pro. I sat in the back of the classroom, keeping to myself when Marissa and Mandy walked up.

The Last Green

"Hey, Colt, did you hear the awesome news?" Mandy asked.

Marissa and Mandy were the coolest girls in the entire middle school. All the boys had a crush on them, including me.

"No, what good news?" I asked sheepishly.

"Didn't you hear Mr. Turner's announcement in the lunchroom?" said Marissa.

I had been in the bathroom with an upset stomach, so I must have missed it.

"No," I answered.

"Our school won some grant, so we get to take a full-day field trip next week," she said.

Nothing was better than a free field trip and a full day out of school.

I perked up. "Cool! Where are we going?"

"Next Friday, we're spending the day at the tram!" Marissa said excitedly.

My heart sank, and in an instant, a blinding headache blindsided me.

"The tram?" I asked, making sure I had heard her correctly.

"Yes, you know, the Palm Springs Aerial Tramway!" Mandy said in a sassy voice.

"Your day is getting better and better. Not only are we all going, but lucky you—you're in our group," Marissa said with a smile.

-13-

The Palm Springs Aerial Tram, the largest rotating aerial tramway in the world, is a world-famous attraction. The tram travels over two and a half miles through the cliffs of Chino Canyon, reaching an elevation of 8,516 feet. The ten-minute ride ascends to the Mountain Station, featuring two restaurants, two theaters, a gift shop, a museum, an observation deck, and 50 miles of hiking in Mt. San Jacinto State Park.

A young engineer named Francis Crocker conceived the idea of the aerial tram in 1935. After years and years of dreaming and planning, the tram finally started moving toward construction in 1950.

During construction, the tram was even labeled the Eighth Wonder of the World. During the construction, helicopters were used due to the ruggedness of the mountain cliffs. Five towers were built spanning the distance to the top of the mountain. Only the first tower was reachable by road.

Crocker's dream was finally completed in 1963. The inaugural ride was filled with local and state dignitaries and celebrities. In 2000, the tram was updated, and passengers were able to ride the world's largest *rotating* tram cars to the top of the mountain and back down to the valley. Since its inception in 1963, over 20 million people have ridden the tram from the base at Valley Station to the top, Mountain Station.

Even though most people enjoyed the thrill and view while riding the tram, I am deathly afraid of it. I hated heights even more than golfing in front of a crowd.

Two years ago, Dad surprised Mom and me with a day off to enjoy Palm Springs. We went shopping downtown and took in all the local sights. The day was great…until we drove to our last exciting event of the day.

Dad turned our car down a side road that led out of the city limits. Driving through the desert was an eerie feeling. I didn't see many houses, and I noticed that we were slowly starting to climb upward. The more we drove, the steeper the road became.

My heart raced. "Where are we going?" I asked.

"It's a surprise," Dad quickly shot back.

I scooted forward, sitting on the edge of my seat to make sure my seat belt was tight. I turned and looked through the back window.

We turned down a winding road, accelerating as the incline increased more and more.

"What are we doing?" I asked in a frantic voice.

Without saying a word, my mom just pointed.

I saw a huge parking lot and the outline of the tram's Mountain Station. As Dad drove closer, I stared in disbelief at our destination.

After had Dad parked the car, I glared at my parents. "I am not going on that thing!" I shouted.

"Son, it's totally safe. You know we would never do anything that would hurt you," responded my dad.

"Let's just go look, Colt," Mom invited. Reluctantly, I opened the car door. The incline was so steep, I had to lean forward to walk up toward the main entrance.

With each step, I felt more and more nauseous. My heart raced as I looked up even higher toward the tram. I watched as the tram took off with a full load of eager, excited people.

As the tram went up, I saw one large black tower outlined against the high cliffs. The tower looked kind of like a large telephone tower or something, but I could tell it had been constructed for the tram's passage.

I noticed a worker sweeping off the steps next to me.

"Sir, is that the top," I asked.

"Where?" he responded.

"That big iron thing," I said as I pointed.

The man started to laugh. "No, no, that's not the

top. That's only the first tower," he replied with a smirk.

I squinted, looking beyond the tower. All I could see was the first tower, and then the steep, mountainous cliffs faded into the fog and clouds.

"That's only the first tower?" I asked in amazement. "How many more towers are there until you reach the top?"

"There are a total of five," he responded.

"Five!" I exclaimed in horror.

The next thing I remembered was waking up in the back of my parents' car. Mom was sitting with me, holding a cold washcloth on my forehead.

I had passed out.

The last thing I remembered was watching the tramcar disappear into the clouds; it looked like it was floating in the sky.

Not unexpectedly, I didn't ride the tram that day. After that, my parents promised me they would never surprise me or talk about going on the tram again. Since that first time, I have been able to avoid that place completely.

Now my nightmare was coming back to haunt me. I would have to face my fear of the tram in front of all my friends and classmates and there was no way could I stay home from school or wimp out on this field trip because this time I was grouped with Marissa and Mandy.

-14-

"Dude, why are you acting like a zombie? We got some golfing to do," said Andy as we waited for my mom to pick us up.

All the talk of the tram had so upset me, I had completely forgotten about golfing with Pro after school.

Now I had both the distress of the tram field trip *and* the pressure of playing with Pro on the same day. My stomach began to ache—much like it did that day two years ago at the tram.

When we got home, we grabbed our golf clubs and jumped on our golf cart. We headed to the clubhouse located next to the #1 tee at Mountain Valley.

I was hoping to get in some putting on the practice green before Pro arrived.

I guess I should have come earlier.

"You boys ready?" he asked as we drove closer.

"You need to ride with Pro," Andy said. I nodded and added my golf clubs to Pro's cart. I was nervous as I sat down next to the golfing legend.

He looked at me and smiled. "We are just playing golf, Colt. There's no need to be nervous; I am only another golfer," he said.

In my mind, Pro was the only person who could take my golf game to a different level.

I was glad we were playing Mountain Valley. I had played the course hundreds of times. I knew every hazard, all the important distances, and the greens.

Pro teed off first and crushed his drive straight and long down the fairway.

I was next.

How am I going to follow that? I asked myself silently.

I took a deep breath, took a practice swing, and

approached the ball. I swung and made good contact. The ball cruised off the tee. I hit it well.

"I didn't get all of it," I quickly said, turning to Pro. I wanted him to know that I could do better; I wanted every shot to be perfect for Pro. I wanted him to see my full potential on every hit.

All he said in response was "Straight is good." Nothing more.

I was hoping he would give me some tips or pointers or at least acknowledge if he thought I had a good hit. I wanted him to build my confidence, so I would know if he wanted to help coach me. Andy and Bob both hit good balls down the fairway.

On the first hole, Pro birdied, and I shot a par. Andy and Bob both bogeyed the hole.

"Good start," I said to myself.

As we continued to the second tee box, I asked Pro about my grip.

"Your grip is fine, Colt. Just golf. Just focus on hitting it straight," he said.

The next three holes were three of my course

favorites. I was two over par after the first four holes. After every shot, I looked to Pro, but he said nothing, offered nothing.

On Hole #5 I lost my drive a little to the right, and the ball landed in some high grass off the fairway. Frustrated, I pounded my driver against the ground.

"You're fine; just keep it in the short grass," he calmly said.

Yeah, that's what I planned on doing, I thought. So far, we were five holes into our game, and Pro hadn't given me any advice or groundbreaking tips. He didn't even give me an indication of whether or not he thought I was a good golfer.

We were just golfing—something I had done for the past six years. I was in awe of Pro. He was three under par after five holes, and he seemingly never made a mistake.

On the fifth hole, Pro missed a 12-foot putt for an eagle. Calmly, he walked over and tapped his ball in for a birdie. He showed no emotion; he was steady and always confident.

We continued to play, and I was even starting to enjoy our time on the course. Pro started warming up to us, mostly because Bob kept probing him with questions. He told us about how he fell in love with his neighbor and high-school sweetheart, his wife Nancy.

The more we played, the better I felt. My confidence was high as we entered the back nine.

On hole #13, a 189-yard par three, I landed a perfect shot that stopped 14 inches from the cup.

"Nice shot, kid," Pro said.

That's the first time he acknowledged one of my shots!

I did notice that Pro was hyper-observant of everything I was doing. He didn't talk much, but he watched intently.

The round couldn't have gone better. I was playing well, and I hoped Pro was impressed. I knew if I hadn't impressed him so far, then I probably wasn't going to. I was happy with how I was playing.

Everything was going great until we approached the tee box on the 17th hole. As we pulled over the hill, I could see a large group of people gathering on the outside deck of the clubhouse restaurant.

"Pro!" someone yelled.

"Hey, Pro! Over here," another said. I could tell by the look on Pro's face he wasn't excited about the crowd's calling his name.

He only half waved to acknowledge the people. Anyone could tell he was slightly annoyed by the appearance of the onlookers.

Pro walked over and quickly hit his tee shot.

I was next. I froze, and the group went quiet but didn't leave.

"Colt, go ahead and hit so we can get out of here," encouraged Pro.

-15-

You're going to shank it, I thought. I shook my head, trying to drive out the negative thoughts. I continued to wrestle mentally with my own thoughts. I turned toward Bob and Andy. With one look at my face, they knew what was happening.

"You're good, Colt! Just don't think about it and hit it. You've been great all day," encouraged Bob.

"You got this," Andy reiterated.

But I knew I didn't have this. I knew I was going to shank it.

I walked up to the tee in a hurry, and without taking a practice swing, I drew back and swung as hard as I could.

I swung so hard, I pulled my head and missed

the entire golf ball. I could hear quiet laughter and snickers from the balcony.

I turned to see the look on Pro's face.

"You're good; just swing nice and smooth," he whispered, trying not to make the moment even more of a disaster.

I knew I wouldn't hit the golf ball solidly. I swung again, this time barely hitting the inside of the ball. The golf ball went about 30 yards before landing in the rough.

"He didn't even hit it past the women's tee," someone snickered.

I was so embarrassed—not just for myself, but for Pro. This golfing legend was out with some kid who was supposed to be a good golfer. If this was tournament play, I would be hitting four already on the hole.

"Guys, let's just go ahead and move on to the 18th," said Pro, walking forward and picking up his golf ball.

A huge sense of relief went through my body. I knew the 18th tee box was hidden from the clubhouse. No one would be watching from a balcony to critique my every swing.

I jumped in the cart with my head down. Pro drove up and leaned over to pick up my golf ball. I could feel my face was still burning red.

He didn't say a word, no motivational speech or any words of wisdom—nothing. I was waiting for him to speak, but he continued driving in silence.

The 18th was a short, 165-yard par three.

Pro walked up and hit a perfect nine iron that landed in the center of the green. I motioned for Bob and Andy to go next. I knew that I shouldn't go after Pro—not after my last tee shot.

Both of the twins hit their balls well. Andy's hit the green and rolled off, and Bob's was just short.

I drew a deep breath, exhaled, walked up, and swung with much more control. My grip wasn't too tight, and I was far more relaxed than I had been at the previous hole. The swing hit the center of the ball as I watched it scream over the pond toward the green. The ball landed and bounced twice, setting up a 20-foot putt for a birdie.

I walked over and got in the cart without saying anything. I barely missed the birdie putt; the ball stopped inches away from the hole.

Pro made his putt; Bob and Andy both three putted for a bogey.

Our round was done, but the game hadn't ended before exposing my biggest flaw to Pro. We shook hands, and I thanked him for golfing with us.

I walked away. No way could I ask Pro to waste his time training me. I had shown him my true colors. *Why would he want to waste his time on me?*

We drove the golf cart up to the clubhouse to unload our clubs. I quickly jumped off and carried my clubs near the putting green where Mom always picked us up.

"Colt, can you meet here tomorrow after school? Around four o'clock?" Pro called from his car.

Surprised by his request, I replied, "Yeah...of course. I'll be here."

-16-

Saturday couldn't come fast enough.

I tried to avoid Marissa and Mandy for the rest of the week, but they finally caught up with me in the lunchroom on Friday.

"Hey, Colt! Are you excited about next Friday?" asked Mandy.

I played it off. "Yeah, should be cool," I said.

"I love the tram!" exclaimed Marissa enthusiastically.

"Me too! It's crazy high!" said Mandy. She was unaware of how petrified I was of heights.

Bob and Andy knew everything about me, especially my fear of heights.

I glanced at the twins, hoping they would bail

me out, but they didn't. They just kept their heads down, eating their lunch.

A small part of me enjoyed the attention I was getting from Marissa and Mandy. I was in their group, and they genuinely seemed excited about it. Every other boy in school would have done anything to be in my position.

"What will you do?" asked Andy.

"You can't bail on Marissa and Mandy! I wish I was in their group; I'm stuck with a bunch of eighth graders I barely know," moaned Bob.

"The tram is no joke. I couldn't believe how high it was at the top," said Andy.

I was already miserable and full of anxiety. My entire world seemed like it was falling apart. I wanted to go back to the days when I didn't have to think about riding the tram or impressing Pro. I didn't want to be afraid of the tram or golfing in front of people. I know to become the type of golfer I wanted to be, I had to find a way to overcome my dread and fear.

I thought about my fearfulness the whole ride

home. My skin ran cold as I glanced out the windows toward the San Jacinto Mountains. How one person can view something as beautiful that horrifies another amazes me. Millions of people loved to ride the tram. I must find a way to get out of having to ride it.

Like it or not, our field trip to the tram was one week away. *If the cable for the tram doesn't snap and send us all to an early grave, I am sure I will have a heart attack and die in front of Marissa and Mandy.* Either way, I didn't see how I would make it past next Friday.

After school I made a beeline toward my mom's car. Mom could tell something major was on my mind. As she drove, she smiled to herself.

When we got home, I went to my room and flopped on my bed. I stared at the ceiling as my thoughts overwhelmed me. *Why must I fear heights? Why can't I be normal like everyone else? Why? Why? Why?* I was totally lost in my own world of self-doubt and worry.

Ten minutes later, I heard the phone ring. Mom

answered, and I could hear her talking become louder as she marched to my room.

The door opened, and Mom said, "It's Tony at the pro shop. He said you're late, and Pro is waiting for you."

Oh, no!

In my distress I had forgotten about my tee time with Pro. I jumped up and ran out the door. I jumped on the golf cart and drove straight toward the clubhouse.

Glancing down at my watch, I noticed it was 4:10 p.m. I was ten minutes late for my four o'clock tee time with Pro. With my mind on the tram ride, I had completely forgotten about my appointment with Pro.

"Will Pro still be there?" I asked myself, pulling into the clubhouse. *Did I spoil this opportunity too?*

-17-

As I pulled around the back side of the clubhouse, I was relieved to see Pro standing with his golf bag by the #1 tee box.

"I'm really sorry," I said, pulling up to load his clubs in my golf cart.

"No worries, Colt. I let a group go ahead of us." Pro was always calm and well-spoken.

"Thanks for golfing with me. I was hoping you could help me with my driver and short irons," I suggested.

Pro turned toward me. "How about we just golf and see what happens?" he asked.

"Oh, yeah. Okay, let's golf," I said, slightly disappointed. I had golfed hundreds of times, but I wanted *lessons* from Pro. I wanted him to correct and help me become a better golfer.

I thought Pro was here to help me fix my golf game.

Pro quickly approached the first tee box and crushed his drive dead center down the fairway.

I followed his shot with a good one of my own.

When we golfed, Pro wasn't into small talk. I'd quickly learned that the last time I golfed with him. I made up my mind, if he wasn't going to tell me how to get better, I would watch him and better myself. I took mental notes every time he swung a club and every time the hit went straight. He seemingly never had a bad shot. Even if the shot wasn't perfect, it was always straight.

Our round was flying by. We were both golfing at a high level and making good shots. Every once in a while Pro would ask me a question, and I noticed that none of them had anything to do with golf.

"Do you like the mountains?" he asked when we reached the 10th green. "Look how gorgeous they are in the background."

The Last Green

On the 15th hole, he asked, "What are your favorite things to do besides golf?"

I was slightly annoyed with the lack of golf-related questions. *This is not how I planned our golf round going.*

I did like the pace of golf we were playing, and I also liked the fact that I was hitting the golf ball solidly. I so badly wanted Pro to see that was a good golfer.

I was sure he was seeing that today.

As we hit onto the 17th green, things started to change. I grabbed my putter and headed toward the green.

As I was lining up my putt, Pro spoke. The fact that he said anything was rare in itself as Pro never talked near the green. After all, the green was a sacred place.

"Colt, after the 18th, I want to introduce you to a really important person who can take your golf game to the next level."

Confused, I turned to stare at him. "I was hoping that you were that person. Did I do something wrong? Why don't you want to be my coach?" I asked honestly.

"That's not it. I will coach you. But just so you know, the last time I took a young golfer under my wing, he chose to move to someone else—someone better than me," he explained.

At this point, it didn't matter. He had just agreed to be my coach and was going to introduce someone else who could help my golf game!

As we putted out on the 18th hole, my mind raced with ideas of who Pro had lined up for me to meet. *Maybe it's Tony!* Tony is a great young golfer; maybe he saw something in my swing that Tony could help me improve.

Or it could be another professional—one of Pro's buddies who lived around Mountain Valley.

Whoever it was, I was anxious to meet that person as we walked toward the clubhouse.

-18-

Pro strolled through the clubhouse, and all the heads turned toward him. I felt like a rock star too. Just being seen with Pro gave me additional credibility on the golf course.

We approached Tony, but he kept walking.

Well, I guess it's not Tony. I followed Pro closely.

We walked into the pro shop.

Pro walked me over to the men's polo shirts and waved for me to stand next to him.

I walked up.

"There, Colt," he said as he pointed. "Right there is the most important person who can help your golf game."

I stood confused. In front of us were racks of

clothing and posters of golfers. I squinted toward one of the posters.

"Him?" I asked, pointing to a poster of some PGA pro promoting a new driver.

"No, not him. Look closer," he instructed.

I looked again, and then I finally realized what Pro meant.

Between the polo shirt racks was a long, rectangular, six-foot mirror. I found myself staring at the one person Pro believed could help my golf game—me. No one else was in the mirror.

"Colt, you are the only one who can help your golf game. You are a fantastic young golfer, but you need to conquer the mental side of the game," he explained.

He added, "You have one of the best swings I have ever seen for someone your age. I can help you with some aspects of the game, but you, Colt, have everything you need to be a champion."

"So, you will help me though?" I asked.

"I will…if you will promise to work on your game—but not just the game on the course. More importantly, you must promise to work on the game between your ears," he said.

We both knew that if I wanted to become the type of golfer we both knew I could be, I had to believe in myself.

"I will appreciate any help you are willing to give me," I said.

"Let's meet every day after school next week; I will set the tee times with Tony. We will start around 4:30 p.m. so you will have enough time to finish any homework before we golf," he said.

I nodded in agreement.

"You should be ready for Saturday," he said with a comforting nod.

"Saturday?" I asked, confused.

"A Junior National Golf Tournament will be held at Trilogy in La Quinta this weekend. I will make sure you're registered," he said.

"This weekend? You think I am ready for a big tournament like that?" I asked.

"You've been ready," he declared, walking out of the clubhouse.

That week, Pro and I golfed every day. We played 18 holes daily. His coaching style was different from any other golf coach with whom I had ever worked.

Pro's approach to coaching was unique. Most of the time he simply watched without commenting. Typically, he waited until the end of each round before commenting. He was big on proper mechanics, putting, and pre-shot routine. He refined my pre-shot routine in a way to ensure that I followed the same routine before every shot. On the putting green, he was amazing at reading the breaks and different greens. I always thought I was good on the greens, but after golfing with Pro, my putting improved tremendously.

He had a gift of teaching me without making me feel like I wasn't a good golfer. His tone was always consistent and confident.

"You'll do great on Saturday," Pro said as we left the 18th green after our Wednesday round.

"You think?" I asked, flipping my golf ball in my hand.

The Last Green

"Yeah, I think you'll win," he said.

"Win? Like the whole tournament?"

"Yep, the whole thing," Pro said.

His confidence in me caused my own self-confidence to soar. I was ready to *play* the Trilogy; I was ready to win at the Trilogy. But then a frightening thought crept into my mind. *I still have one issue—the one part of my game we haven't worked on or fixed.*

Golfing with Dad, Bob, Andy, or even Pro had never been an issue. I always played well with a small number of other people.

I knew any golf tournament, especially one like the Trilogy, would have a large number of spectators. All the lessons in the world didn't seem to help that situation—even lessons from Pro. My newfound confidence faded as I lifted my clubs off the cart.

Fear and thoughts of failing took the place of all those happy, confident feelings I had while golfing with Pro. I had just played a great round of golf, but doubt was starting to take over once again.

"Colt, come here. I have something for you—a small gift that will help you tomorrow," said Pro as he reached for his golf bag.

-19-

Pro leaned over and unzipped a side pocket. I couldn't see what was in it, but he had grabbed something out of the small compartment.

As he turned and held out his hand, I opened mine. He dropped a weathered golf tee into the palm of my hand.

"This is one of my lucky golf tees. Put this in your pocket and feel it when you get nervous. It'll remind you to stay calm," he said.

Did he use this when he played in one of his major golf tournaments? Maybe he used it in the Masters or U.S. Open.

Wherever he had used this tee, it had to be important coming from Pro. I held the tee in my hand, examining it one more time before securing it in my right pants pocket.

"Thanks," I said. "I hope it works!" I smiled nervously.

"It only works if you believe it will," he said slyly.

I rubbed my pocket, feeling the sharp bottom of the tee. *Strange, but I do feel different and more confident with my new lucky tee.*

The next morning came quickly. I met Pro at the Trilogy for the first day of the two-day golf tournament. In this tournament, coaches weren't allowed to be with the golfers.

I felt nervous not to have Pro next to me, but I knew he would follow me on every hole. Plus, I had his lucky golf tee in my pocket. I made sure when I was getting ready this morning that I had stuffed the tee into my golfing pants.

I was ranked twenty-eighth out of the sixty golfers at the tournament. The top three finishers would earn a spot at next week's Best of the West Junior National Championship hosted by PGA West. Only the top junior golfers played in the Best of the West. Last year, my dad had taken me, and I was amazed at how good the young golfers were. I would love to play in that tournament, but I knew my chances of finishing in the top three was slim.

This tournament was my first Junior PGA event, so I knew others had played in previous tournaments, giving them a higher ranking. The knowledge gave me a small amount of added confidence because I knew I had beat them.

The Trilogy is a beautiful course, and the weather was perfect. At eight o'clock in the morning, the temperatures were in the mid-70s, and a slight breeze was blowing from the northwest.

On the first day, I was paired with a nice kid named Luke who was around my age. He was from nearby Cathedral City.

Parents, spectators, and coaches had to stay behind roped-off boundary lines. Before teeing off on hole #1, I looked over my right shoulder to see Pro and my dad in the crowd.

I smiled and rubbed my hand over my right pocket, feeling Pro's tee.

Hole #1 was a 378-yard par 4 that had a slight dogleg left.

Luke hit the first shot—a nice straight drive that flew about 210 yards and rolled. His was a good starting shot.

But I knew I could blow past his ball.

I took a long, slow, steadying breath and a practice swing. I used the exact same pre-shot routine Pro had shown me. "Just hit it straight, and if you miss, miss it straight," I told myself.

Pro had engrained this advice in me over and over the past two weeks. He wanted my focus to be on the shot and not all the dangers around it.

I stepped up to the tee, pulled back and swung hard and confidently. My driver hit the ball solidly, and I watched as it exploded down the fairway.

I had hammered it! The ball landed 30 yards past Luke's ball and rolled another 10 or so yards. I had outdriven him by over 50 yards.

"Wow! You smoked that," Luke exclaimed, turning back to me.

I also blasted my second shot. My iron shot was

true as the ball bounced within two feet of the cup, setting me up for an easy birdie putt.

I was off to a great start—a championship beginning.

-20-

My confidence soared as I calmly tapped in the birdie putt.

I turned back toward the crowd and made eye contact with Pro. Dad was gleaming. I could see he was proud of me and excited.

Pro had a different look. His eyes were steady and relaxed. I could tell that I was doing what he expected me to do. Though I saw no fanfare in his eyes, I still saw what I needed to see—his confidence in me.

He would save the clapping and congratulations until the end. After all, golf is not a sport that is won on the first hole.

The rest of the morning, I played consistent

golf. I was straight off the tee, and my short game was sharp. On several holes I ended up three putting, which hurt my overall score.

Luke was a good golfer, but he had nowhere near my ability. He was seven over heading into the 18th tee. I was three under par, which meant I was ten strokes better than him on the first day.

Hole #18 is 517 yards and a difficult par-5 hole. Luke was struggling with his driver.

"You got this, Luke. Finish strong," I said to him as we drove toward the 18th.

"Thanks, man. I don't know though. I am not hitting well today," he said.

"You got this," I replied.

As we pulled over the hill next to the 18th hole, my heart dropped.

A large crowd had gathered to watch the tournament. Many of the golfers who had finished before us were standing around the hole, watching everyone finish their rounds.

Luke noticed the look on my face and asked, "You okay, Colt?"

"I'm good," I said, trying to play it off.

I had the lower score on the previous hole, so that meant that I would be teeing off first.

I grabbed my driver and walked toward the tee box. My hands started to sweat, and my knees were suddenly weak. I had played well enough to position myself as a contender in the tournament. Now I had one hole left for the day, and I knew I had to finish strong on the last green of the day.

I took a practice swing, and nothing felt right. My grip was too tight, and my swing felt heavy and awkward. "Just look at the people," I said to myself. *They're all watching and waiting for me to mess up!*

All eyes seemed to be fixed on this young golfer from La Quinta. I backed off the tee box uncomfortable with my practice swing.

"Clear your head, Colt. Remember your routine," I said to myself.

Then my hand bumped my right pocket. The rough wooden edge of my lucky golf tee poked through my pocket. My golf tee! I smiled, remembering my good luck charm Pro had gifted me.

The Last Green

I drew back and swung hard.

I watched as my golf ball blasted off the tee toward the fairway.

I walked back and slumped back into the golf cart relieved I had survived a potential meltdown. *I did it! I managed to hit a good shot off the tee box in front of a big crowd!*

I ended up with a birdie on the hole, which put me at four under par after the first round of the tournament.

I shook hands with Luke, and we complimented each other on our golf match.

I fist bumped Pro and my dad as I walked into the clubhouse to turn in my official scorecard.

I handed it to the official at the registration table and waited.

I watched in amazement as they walked up and put my name on the leaderboard—in striking distance of the first-place golfer!

I was in sixth place and only down two strokes from the overall leader who was sitting at six under par.

For the first time I had taken my negative self-talk and doubt head-on and won!

Little did I know my long war with my self-confidence had only just begun.

Tomorrow was going to be a big day!

-21-

That night Bob and Andy sat in the swimming pool listening to every word about my golf match.

"Sounds like you played awesome, Colt," Bob declared.

"Trilogy is a tough course; you must have been hitting the ball well," Andy chipped in.

They had played Trilogy before and knew all the holes as I recapped my round with them.

"When I got to the 18th fairway, loads of people were there to watch," I mentioned.

Andy stopped laughing and looked at me with wide eyes. They were both well aware of my issues with crowds and my lack of confidence.

"And?" he impatiently asked when I paused.

"I hit a bomb off the tee straight down the fairway!" I said with a smile.

"Finally! I have been telling you for years to stop melting down when people show up," said Bob.

I smiled. *I knew I had conquered my lack of confidence that day...but could I in the future?*

Then I told them about the special tee that Pro had given me.

"I bet that was a tee he used when he hit one of his nine holes in one," said Andy.

"Or it could be the tee he used when he made the cut and played in Augusta during the Masters Tournament," said Bob.

"I'm not sure, but I do know it's special. If I have that tee, I'll be good," I said.

After a couple of hours, the twins got up to go home. I had to go to bed early to prepare for tomorrow's important round of golf.

Andy stopped before shutting the front door behind him. "You still got that tee, right?" he asked.

"Of course, it's in a safe place," I said with a grin.

And it was. The tee was zipped in a special side

pocket of my golf bag. Nothing else was in that pocket, and I had zipped it tightly. *No way am I losing that tee!*

That night I went to bed dreaming of golf. I closed my eyes and replayed the drive I hit on the 18th box.

I knew that if I played as well as I had today, I would make the top ten, which would be a huge accomplishment for my first Junior Tour event.

That night I slept well. I went to bed early and woke up ready to play another 18 holes of golf at Trilogy. The tournament was scheduled over two days, and everyone knew that Sunday was championship day. Saturday gave golfers a chance to get into the championship, but championships were played for and won on Sunday.

I had 18 holes left to play. If the next day went as well as today, I would finish in the top ten and medal.

I had no way of knowing that I wasn't going to play as well as I had yesterday.

-22-

Sunday morning was the beginning of a gorgeous California day.

Dad took me to the golf course early so I could loosen up and hit some practice balls on the driving range. My tee time was at 8:30 a.m., but we arrived around seven o'clock. I wanted to make sure I had plenty of time to warm up and practice my putting before the spectators started to arrive.

Pro had beaten me there once again.

Pro loved everything about golf. The mornings were his favorite time to be on the course. He liked to be there before all the fanfare and people arrived.

We shared that love.

"Good to see you, Colt. Glad you're taking today seriously," he said.

"Yes, I am," I said.

I was proud of how I had played yesterday. Seeing my name toward the top of the leaderboard at the Trilogy had gotten me even more excited.

"What's the plan for today?" questioned Pro.

"Play good golf," I replied, not sure what I was supposed to say. I wanted to say more about winning, but I didn't want to come off as being overly confident. "Finish in the top ten," I added.

Pro smiled. "Let's just keep it in the short grass, Colt. If you do that, everything else will take care of itself."

Pro loved to make statements without saying specifically what he meant. But after spending time with him the past two weeks, I knew exactly what he meant. Pro placed a lot of emphasis on hitting the ball straight. "You won't have to worry about hazards, going out-of-bounds, or other golfers—if you can keep it straight," he said.

One of the things I had noticed the first time I

golfed with Pro was that every shot was straight. Even if he didn't hit the ball super far, the drive was always straight.

I headed to the driving range, and Pro watched me hit some balls. He gave me little tips that made an immediate impact, like pointing out that my wrist was in the wrong spot or that I wasn't transferring my weight well off the tee.

"I really like what I'm seeing today, Colt," Pro said as I hit the last ball in my bucket. The driving range was starting to fill up with other golfers now. And every golfer who arrived knew that I had been there early.

I was prepared to win.

My confidence was at an all-time high as we headed out to hole #1. My swing was smooth, and my lucky tee was perched safely in my pocket.

I was seeded in the top group with three other great golfers.

I watched as my first three opponents confidently stepped up to the tee box on hole #1 and hit long, straight drives.

The Last Green

I was the last of our foursome to tee off.

I stepped back, took a couple of practice swings, and lined up my shot.

My ball bounced and rolled, stopping 20 yards ahead of the farthest golf ball. The huge drive was so good, each golfer turned and quickly looked back at me. I had their attention now.

There was no doubt I belonged in this group. They knew it, but more importantly, so did I.

By the time the front nine had been completed, I was tied for first at 8 under par with a kid out of the Los Angeles area. The second-place golfer was sitting at 4 under.

This tournament is mine to win.

I just had to finish strong.

-23-

In the game of golf, seemingly nothing goes right some days, and the game destroys you mentally. Then there are days, though few and far between, that make you feel like you own the game. Some golfers refer to it as being "in the zone."

That was where I was on the back nine of the Trilogy. Every shot felt pure and powerful.

Instead of melting under the pressure, I became stronger. The entire tournament came down to the last hole—the 18th hole.

The par 5, 520-yard hole was a nemesis for most people. For most golfers, ending on a long par 5 was not ideal. By then, fatigue and the difficulty of the course had usually caught up with them.

The Last Green

The long yardage of the hole was good for me. I had been blasting my driver all day and looked forward to ending on the par five 18th hole.

I had a one-stroke lead heading into the final hole.

My tee shot went straight, landing about 250 yards down the fairway. For my second shot, I grabbed my 5-wood and gave it a solid swing though I knew I couldn't drive the green from there. I simply wanted to set up my third shot, and the ball landed about 50 yards from the center of the green, giving me a perfect third shot.

My opponent, feeling the pressure of trying to make up a stroke, grabbed his 3-wood. I could tell when he approached the ball that his swing wouldn't be good. His grip was so tight, he would have to hit the ball with everything he had to land it on the green.

His swing was fast and furious, and I watched as his golf ball sliced wildly, landing in a deep sand trap to the left of the fairway. He was lucky, and if the ball hadn't hit the sand trap, it would have been hit out of bounds. I watched as he angrily slammed down his club.

He knew what everyone else knew.

All I had to do was hit a nice pitch shot onto the green and two-putt for the win.

His next shot out of the sand trap was amazing, landing about 20 yards behind my ball. He approached it and pitched it onto the back of the green. I knew from that location he would at least two-putt.

My pitch shot landed somewhat short of where I wanted but still rolled up onto the green. His next putt was a long lag putt. I knew he didn't expect to make that long putt, but he had hopes of getting close to the cup. Unbelievably, his ball stopped about 15 feet from mine.

I surveyed the green and could see a slight break to the left near the end of the cup. My putter felt heavy in my hands. I backed off the ball and drew in a deep breath. I steadied my hands and resorted back to my thousands of hours of training.

Without even thinking, I reached back and hit

the ball. The golf ball twisted and turned toward the cup before falling into the hole.

The large crowd that had gathered to watch the game went crazy.

I grabbed my ball and walked over to the side of the green, allowing my competitor to finish. He putted and missed, then walked up and tapped his ball in.

I had won first place in the tournament!

I felt the strong arms of my dad grabbing me from behind. His face beamed with excitement as he hugged me.

Pro pulled me close, giving me a rare hug. I knew he liked me, but I also knew he wasn't a very emotional person. He started patting my back and nodding.

"That a boy, Colt. That a boy!" he said.

I walked into the clubhouse and handed one of the tournament directors my scorecard. I watched as he walked up to the leaderboard and placed my name at the top.

Since our group had been in the lead, we were

the last golfers on the course. Now we huddled eagerly around the announcer waiting for the final results.

"What an excellent display of young golfers we had on the course this weekend," the emcee announced. "I'm sure that you're going to see some of these kids on the PGA Tour someday."

I waited with anticipation as they announced the top ten finishers.

"Placing first overall is La Quinta's own Colt Taylor!" he boomed.

The crowd cheered as I walked forward to receive a huge trophy and held it as a bunch of people took pictures. My ear-to-ear smile was huge and uncontrollable.

After a couple minutes of handshakes and high-fives from random people, I saw the tournament director approaching. "Colt, congratulations," he said, smiling and shaking my hand.

"Thank you, sir," I quickly responded.

"Here, you're going to need this," he said, handing me a white manila envelope.

The Last Green

"What's this?" I asked, confused.

"By winning today, you automatically qualified for next week's Best of the West Junior Golf Tournament at PGA West," he said.

-24-

The PGA Best of the West Junior Golf Tournament was one of the biggest golf tournaments in the world. Kids aged 12 and under traveled from all over the country to play in this tournament which aired on local television. The Golf Network even showed clips of plays throughout the tournament. This tournament was a big deal.

"Don't think about that now; just enjoy the win," Pro whispered in my ear.

I nodded. *Enjoying my win is exactly what I plan to do.* I walked out with the gigantic trophy. I buckled in the front passenger side of Dad's car, holding it.

I waved goodbye to Pro as we headed home. I

couldn't wait to relive my win with my mom and the twins. Mom even made a celebratory dinner of steak and mashed potatoes—my all-time favorite.

As soon as we pulled in the driveway, I saw Bob and Andy sitting on my front porch, anxiously awaiting our arrival.

Their eyes brightened, and they jumped up with excitement as we stopped. I struggled to get my seat belt off as they sprinted toward the car.

I rattled the handle, opening the door just in time to thrust my arms and trophy high in the air before being mobbed by them.

"You did it, man! You did it!" yelled Bob.

"We are so proud! Our best friend is the tournament champion!" Andy exclaimed.

"Thanks, guys! I couldn't have done it without you both. Your confidence and all those rounds we played this summer helped me a ton," I declared.

The boys quickly waved to Dad and took off to grab their swimsuits.

I went inside and grabbed Mom in a tight hug. "Colt, I'm so proud of you. I knew you were the best golfer there. Dinner can wait while you go swim with the twins."

"Thanks, Mom!" I rushed to my room to change.

When we went swimming, the twins and I always played a game of sorts. Whoever was the first one to cannonball in the pool, wins.

I reached for the handle to the sliding door just as I heard a huge splash from the swimming pool. For like the hundredth time in a row, Bob had beaten us all once again. His cannonball was followed by two more, as Andy and I jumped in.

We laughed and goofed around for a while before Bob started asking questions about the tournament.

"What did it feel like to hold that trophy in front of everyone?" he asked curiously.

"I'm not going to lie; it felt pretty awesome," I said, unable to stop a smile from covering my face.

I quickly added, "But get this! It gets even better! I qualified to play in the Best of the West next weekend."

"No way!" Bob shouted.

The Last Green

"Are you serious? You do know who's playing in that tournament, don't you?" Andy quickly asked.

I didn't realize that Andy wasn't really asking me a question. As I started to answer him, he interrupted me. "Brady Matthew is coming."

Brady Matthew was the #1 ranked 12-year-old golfer in the world. Anyone who knew anything about golf knew who Brady was.

Last spring, ESPN had produced a full feature story on Brady, calling him the next golfing prodigy, even projecting he would be "the next hottest golf prospect."

Brady had also been featured on the cover of *Sports Illustrated* when he was only ten years old. A sports reporter followed Brady, highlighting his extreme training schedule in the feature article. The kid lived to play golf, starting when he was only four years old. His dad was an avid golfer and took Brady out almost every day. From that exposure, Brady fell in love with the game, especially the mechanics of hitting the ball.

His swing was one of the most natural swings

I had ever seen. Stories about Brady were well-known and traveled around the United States. The news feature included the story of him beating the club champion at his home course when he was only ten years old.

Bob and Andy's dad had bought tickets to the event so the boys could see him in person. Bob even had cut out the *Sports Illustrated* article and posted it on the wall of his room.

"Cool…now I get to play in the same tournament as the great Brady Mathew," I muttered under my breath.

I had been so excited and wrapped up in the moment of winning, I didn't even think about the pressure of playing in the tournament. Celebrities would be attending the tournament, not to mention the event would be televised.

Suddenly, all the fun and excitement drained right out of me. I abruptly remembered something else that was happening this week.

I will have to face two of my greatest fears. How can I do that?

-25-

"Colt, you know what we are doing on Friday?" Andy asked.

I nodded. I knew, and I was trying not to think about it. This coming Thursday, two days before the biggest golf junior tournaments in the world, I had a field trip to the Palm Springs Aerial Tramway.

"You don't have to go. I mean, if it's that scary, just stay home," Bob said.

He quickly added with a wink, "I'll be glad to take your place right next to Mandy and Marisa."

"I have to go. I can't wimp out, and I don't see any way out," I groaned.

I smiled through dinner and enjoyed having

Bob and Andy by my side. We had a great night, but in the back of my mind, I knew that Friday was quickly approaching.

After everyone went home, I rested in bed, staring at the ceiling. *What if I get sick the morning of the field trip? Can I talk to my teacher and tell her about my fear of heights? Would she let me stay at the bottom of the mountain?*

If I had learned anything from Pro over the past week, it was to face my fears head-on. I could've easily folded on the 18th hole at Trilogy. Before meeting Pro Kitchen, I probably would have lost it and melted.

But I didn't. Pro had instilled the belief, but I had to believe too. And I did.

But this situation was vastly different. I hated heights! More than anything on earth, my fear of heights was real. Bob and Andy knew that on my first and only encounter with the tram that I had passed out even before boarding. *I can't show my fear in front of the girls...*

An awful junior-high drama was starting to

play out in my mind. *What if I passed out when I was next to Mandy and Marisa?*

Being embarrassed in front of the coolest girls in the entire school was a real-life nightmare. My mind raced between visions of the tram and playing at PGA West.

Somehow, I knew I had to find a way to overcome both of my biggest fears within two days of each other.

After what felt like forever, I finally drifted off to sleep. I barely slept that night, but when I woke up, I had a good solution to my problem.

I knew every day after school I'd be practicing and working on the golf course with Pro. So, during that time, I would need to focus only on golf. I couldn't let myself lose focus. I knew that Pro would help give me a good perspective on how to handle the pressure of the Best of the West tournament, and I'd have to do my best to stay present during our lessons.

My top priority for the moment was to focus on surviving the tram ride without embarrassing myself. Maybe I'd just take my lucky tee that had saved me so many times already.

Why wouldn't it work on the tram as well?

-26-

I practiced with Pro longer and harder than I ever had before. We were working on my short game and starting to prepare me for the greens at LaQuinta's PGA West, located in the epicenter of Palm Springs, consisting of nine different golf courses. Every hole boasts a spectacular view, as well as multiple challenging tee boxes.

PGA West, which is unlike any golf course in the world, was built by the best of the best. The architects of PGA West were some of the biggest names, as well as the best in the golf business, including Arnold Palmer, Jack Nicklaus, Greg Norman, Tom Weiskopf and Pete Dye.

The two-day tournament took place on both of

the courses designed by Pete Dye. On Saturday, the golfers played the Mountain Course. Competitors start at the base of the breathtaking Santa Rosa Mountains. The terrain is tough, featuring pot bunkers, rock formations and elevated tee boxes.

Championship Sunday was played at the historical, world-famous Stadium Course. Besides being rated as a Top 100 course, it's also ranked in the top 50 toughest courses in America. The course was regularly featured on television and the Golf Channel. The Stadium Course also hosts the PGA Tour "Q-School" for amateur golfers trying to earn their tour card.

In 1987 Lee Trevino hit one of the most unforgettable hole-in-one shots in PGA history during the Skins Game on the Stadium Course's Hole #17, also known as Alcatraz. The shot earned him $175,000 and was listed as one of golf's greatest moments.

I felt fortunate to be part of such an honorable tradition of playing at PGA West. The course wasn't far from our house, but I had never played there.

The Last Green

Thankfully, Pro had played the course six times over the span of his career and knew the course.

He shared his biggest warning with me on Wednesday night as we were on the practice putting green at Mountain View. "Don't get lured in by the scenery and terrain," he cautioned.

"Get lured in?" I questioned.

"Yeah. The views are spectacular, but they're also very intimidating. You will face times of teeing off on tight fairways, and other times you will be surrounded by rocks and mountains," Pro explained and then added, "Don't let yourself get overwhelmed by the hazards and all that can go wrong."

"I'll try," I said hesitantly, trying to imagine what PGA West looked like.

"My last piece of advice is simple: when you're surrounded by danger and hazards, just…"

I quickly interrupted Pro. "Keep it straight. I know, I know, if I miss on my swing, just miss straight," I said with a smile.

"I think you're finally ready, Colt," Pro said.

-27-

Toward the end of our practice session, I became apprehensive, feeling tense, and my body started to stiffen. Pro could tell something was going on.

"Colt, listen to me. You got this. Just the fact that you were invited to play in the Best of the West is a big deal. Don't put too much pressure on yourself; simply try to enjoy playing at that level of golf," he said softly.

"Thanks, I appreciate that advice," I told him.

"What's on your mind? Is there anything else I can help you with?" he asked.

"Well…how do you feel about heights?" I asked.

"I love them! The higher, the better," he added.

"I guess you can't help me with anything else today then." I shrugged.

The next day was the tram field trip, and I still hadn't thought of a way to be excused from going.

I returned to putting practice, but my focus was gone, and my putting was terrible.

"Colt, we're good for today. We still have two days for practice. We'll do more putting on Friday," Pro assured me.

I packed up my gear and drove the golf cart back home. I pulled in as the sun was going down.

I turned toward the Santa Rosa Mountains and admired their sheer beauty. The mountains cut through the orange sky perfectly. The gorgeous, surreal-looking backdrop almost looked fake. I imagined that PGA West, with its incredible scenery, would have a similar effect on me. *How could something so beautiful be so many other things at the same time?*

Today, I was safely staring at the majestic mountains, but tomorrow I would be thousands of feet high, looking down into the valley.

I was too embarrassed to bring up my fear of the tram to Pro. My fear of heights was something I didn't want other people to know about, especially him. He seemed so calm and fearless. I thought back to my dad's stories about how Pro fought against injustice—even in the face of intimidating consequences like losing his sponsorships. *I wish I had that kind of radical courage.*

I was partially able to contain my fear of golfing in front of large crowds, but I didn't have any answers to my fear of the tram.

That night, as I rested in bed, I tried not to think about Saturday's golf tournament or my fear of heights. Unfortunately, my mind kept jumping to the dark, negative place of my horrible experience at the tram two years earlier.

I turned on some music and reached to my nightstand for Pro's lucky tee. The last time I looked at my alarm clock next to my bed, it read 1:05 a.m.

The next morning was rough as I struggled to wake up. I was tired from going to bed so late and anxious for the field trip to be over. My stomach hurt and twisted as I sat down for breakfast. Mom made waffles and bacon, usually my favorite breakfast.

She noticed something was off as I sat staring at the food.

"Colt, are you okay?" she asked.

"I'm fine," I replied tensely.

"You don't look fine," Mom said, with a concerned look on her face. Then she quickly added, "Is this about the golf tournament?"

"No, I'm trying not to think about that. Today my class is taking a field trip to ride the tram…"

"Oh? Why didn't you tell me about that earlier?" she questioned.

"I had Dad sign the permission slip last week. I don't like to talk about the tram; it seems to make things worse," I said.

"Sometimes talking can help, Son. You know I'm always here for you."

I knew Mom was right, and I did want to talk to her and tell her how I was feeling.

"I know the tram isn't something you enjoy."

"Mom, that's putting it nicely. I'm scared out of my mind," I whispered.

"Sometimes, Son, you must put faith in front of your fear. Yes, fear is scary. I get it, but faith says it's all going to be okay," she said.

"I know, Mom."

"Your dad and I would never let you do something if we thought there was any danger, or you could get seriously hurt. You know that, Colt."

Even though I knew millions of people visit the tram every year without falling to their deaths, I simply couldn't shake the feeling of doom. My mind was filled with scenarios. *There's always a first time for everything. What if the day we're there is the day something tragic and horrible happens? What if some silly eighth grader hits the wrong button, the tram door opens, and spills all of us on the rocks below?*

I know no one ever plans an accident; that's why they're called *accidents*. Mom's pep talk, which was meant to encourage me, left me feeling even more worried.

The Last Green

My legs started to shake as I grabbed my backpack off my bed. I reached down to grab the wad of cash that Dad had given to me earlier. *Hopefully, I live long enough to spend it.*

As we backed out of our driveway, a strange thought popped into my mind. I couldn't help but wonder if I would ever see my house again.

-28-

The classroom buzzed with energy and excitement as every eighth grader at William Taft Middle School celebrated a day free from school.

As I walked into class, I felt a hand grab my arm.

"You good?" Bob asked, concerned.

"Colt, it's okay if you don't go. You don't have to prove anything to anyone," Andy quickly followed up.

"Do I look scared?" I quickly asked.

"You look okay—definitely not great, but not petrified," Bob answered.

I can work with that.

The fact that I had passed out the last time I visited the tram was something I didn't want to become public knowledge. I had no plans on repeating the incident—at least that's what I kept telling myself.

Our teacher took attendance, and we loaded onto a school bus to go to the Palm Springs Aerial Tram. I sat with Bob and Andy on the bus. The bus was crazy and loud, but our shared seat was quiet. Bob and Andy knew there was nothing we could discuss. They understood I had to face the tram and talking about it only made the coming experience worse.

After about 20 minutes, the bus driver turned, taking an obscure and isolated road.

The bus was obviously starting to climb, taking the ascent toward the tram. The front of the bus was pointed up the mountain while the back was angled straight down. The incline was so intense, I felt the weight of gravity forcing my head back onto the seat. I knew we were even closer.

The road grew steeper as the bus continued to creep upward. My body started to react to my severe anxiety. My palms started sweating, and my skin went cold. I felt like my heart was going to beat right out of my chest.

After a couple of winding turns, the front of the bus once again pointed upward. In the distance, I could see parking lots and the outline of the Valley Station, a large building to hold crowds of visitors.

We're there. I turned and looked over my shoulder behind us. The distance we had already climbed to reach the base of the tram shocked me! *We've already come higher than I have ever wanted to be—without even stepping foot on the aerial tram!*

The parking lots were starting to fill up with people, so we had to park the bus in Lot F. As we unloaded off the bus, I did my best to avoid looking at the tram.

Before leaving the school, our teachers had efficiently prearranged the classes into groups so we could begin loading immediately. As we started the climb up the steep incline toward the Valley Station, I had to lean forward with all my weight to make the walk.

I was assigned to group C, and Bob and Andy

were in group D right after me. I knew a couple of the other kids in my group but planned on hanging with Marissa and Mandy—if I didn't pass out or throw up on them. I was a tad surprised to find that I wasn't as shaky as I had been the first time.

I knew the girls were watching me. Maybe that attention was all the extra motivation my body needed to perform properly.

All the boys in my class were jealous that I was in group C because that meant that I was the one spending the day with Marissa and Mandy.

We worked our way through the ticket line, and headed toward the boarding gate. The lines were long, which made me happy. As I stood in line, I smiled and acted like everything was wonderful.

Slowly but surely, the line moved forward. When we got closer, the view opened up toward the mountains and gave way to the tram cars as they ascended.

The barrier of fog that was slowly starting to lift still prevented me from seeing the top of the mountains.

As we came closer to boarding the tram, my view changed, and I could now see directly up the mountain. When I turned and looked upward, my knees went weak. I had to reach out and grab the handrail to keep from going down. I stared upward toward the top of the mountain.

This time I could see through the fog. In the far distance, I saw the two transfer locations that looked like telephone wires. The last one looked very tiny. I could see only the two, which meant three more were still unseen.

It's so high—so much higher than I remember!

-29-

The Palm Springs Aerial Tramway is the largest rotating aerial tramway in the world. Opened in 1963, the ride was designed to take passengers from the floor of the Coachella Valley to the top of the San Jacinto Mountains.

In 2000 the 18-foot-in-diameter tram cars were updated to slowly revolve, making two complete rotations during the journey to the top of the mountain. Each car can hold up to 80 passengers.

The twelve-and-a-half-minute ride begins at the Valley Station at 2,643 feet. From there, the tram travels up the sheer mountain edge covering five different life zones on its way to the Mountain Station at 8,526 feet above sea level.

On a clear day at the Mountain Station, visitors can see for 200 miles and can locate Mount Charleston in Nevada. The views are spectacular.

"Sir, how many of those t-like poles are there?" I asked an older man who was checking our tickets.

"Oh, those transfer stations? Before reaching the top, you will see a total of five," he said with a pleasant smile.

He bent down as if he wanted to tell me a secret.

"Wait till you feel what it's like when you hit them; it's a crazy feeling," he whispered.

My heart sank to my stomach. I could make out two of the stations before the tram disappeared into the sky. *Five? Did he actually say five?*

Our group was the next to board the tram. I turned back to see Bob and Andy behind me. I had hoped somehow their group would ride with mine. Just having the twins near me would have helped. I started counting kids and stopped at 70, as I could see a ton of kids still between us. I knew there was no way the twins would be riding with me on the same tram.

The Last Green

The sounds and hustle around me quieted, and I was alone with my own disastrous thoughts.

"You ready?" I heard from beside me, shocking me back into reality.

I turned to see Marissa.

"Oh, yeah, for sure," I said.

"Good, because to be honest with you, I'm slightly terrified. Knowing you're not makes me feel better," she said with a wink.

At least I'm not the only one scared. Maybe we can pass out together.

We started to board the tram, and my heart began to race even faster.

I walked toward the middle of the car and tightly grasped the railing. I had no desire to look out the windows of the tram. Somehow, in all the hustle to board the tram, Marissa and Mandy were separated from me. They ended up on the outside of the tram facing the windows.

I'm so glad I'm not with them.

A thousand frantic thoughts ran through my mind; I searched for any valid excuses that could get me off this death trap. My best idea was that I could tell them I had to go to the bathroom, get off, and hide in the gift shop all day. I knew that plan wouldn't work, though, as a day of activity had been planned at the Mountain Station. But the idea of spending any amount of time that high in the air made me lightheaded and unsteady.

I started to back up slowly, inching my way back toward the exit door. I didn't know what I was going to say or do. I only knew that I couldn't ride this contraption up the mountain. I kept an eye on the girls; they were looking out the window, paying no attention to me. *Maybe I can save my dignity...*

As I was about to exit, a rush of people entered the tram, pushing me back toward the middle.

I struggled back toward the exit right when the door started to close. I reached for the exit handle and missed.

Suddenly, I felt two cold hands lock onto my arm!

-30-

I turned in absolute panic as the doors slammed shut. *I'm locked in the tram! I have nowhere to run or to hide.*

I ripped my arm away and spun to see who had grabbed me. To my relief, Bob and Andy were standing there, grinning from ear to ear.

"How did you guys get on?' I asked in disbelief.

Andy looked and motioned toward Bob. "You know Bob can talk anyone into anything!"

"It was no big deal, Colt. I just might not have enough money for any souvenirs," he answered with his famous smile.

Friendship is a special relationship. I know that I'm lucky to have these two in my corner.

We worked our way back toward the center of the tram. Thankfully, we were able to grab the middle railing. I thought not being able to see how high we were going might help me.

The comfort of having Bob and Andy with me was enough to keep me from passing out, but I was still scared out of my mind. I closed my eyes and tried not to think about where I was.

When I opened my eyes, I felt a slight jerk as the tram started ascending to the top of the mountain. I squinted my eyes shut as tightly as possible.

I tried to convince myself that twelve-and-a-half minutes isn't that long. I tried to think of happy thoughts as the tram worked its way up the steep rocky edge of the mountain.

"Please hold on, as we are approaching the first transfer station," announced the tram operator.

Hold on? If I hold on any tighter, I will break my fingers.

Then it happened…the tram suddenly went up and down, rocking back and forth. I felt like the car was unattached, floating in the air.

The Last Green

This is it; we're going down.

I truly believed that the tram was plummeting downward until I felt the car stabilize. Even though I had been warned that the transfer would cause a crazy feeling, I wasn't totally prepared. I felt my stomach turning, and my heart pounding.

"Ladies and gentlemen, we have now passed Transfer Station #1…only four more to go," the speaker announced.

We are only one fifth of the way to the top, and I still have to survive four more transfer stations.

"I don't think I can do it," I whispered.

"Yes, Colt! Yes, you can! You're doing it," Andy reassured me.

"Dude, don't look out the windows; trust me," said Bob.

A couple of minutes later, the operator announced we were approaching transfer station #2. I gripped the bar, thankful for knowing a little more what was about to happen. I was more prepared when we hit the transfer, but the jostling still felt strange and sudden.

I let go of the railing but only long enough to wipe the sweat from my eyes…and made a huge mistake. I peeked over Bob's shoulder. *We're floating so high in the sky!*

As I stretched my hand toward the center railing, I hit something in my pocket. In the wad of cash I had grabbed from my nightstand was my lucky golf tee. I squeezed it tightly and prepared myself for the next transfer station.

Pro's special golf tee will calm my fear and save me from the tram. I pulled it out of my pocket and squeezed it as hard as I could.

-31-

The fourth transfer was by far the roughest. I felt the bottom of the tram swing wildly as my stomach went into my throat. I steadied my body, then attempted a deep breath before raising my eyes to take a quick peek. This time I looked over Andy's shoulder down toward the valley.

I couldn't believe my eyes. The Valley Station looked like the size of a matchbox car. My face flushed, and I stumbled. Bob's hand squeezed my arm, stabilizing me.

We still had one more transfer station before we reached the top. *This ride has been the longest twelve-and-a-half minutes of my life.*

I knew we had to be close. I rearranged my

grip and closed my eyes as the tram operator announced the fifth and final transfer.

When we passed the station, the car leveled out. My eyes were still closed as we rocked back and forth. I didn't want to open my eyes, but I knew something was different. We leveled out as the tram continued upward. A couple more minutes passed before I heard the operator's voice say, "Welcome to the Mountain Station!"

Everyone cheered. Well, almost everyone. I didn't have enough strength to cheer, but I was filled with joy and incredibly relieved.

I limped off the tram and went over to sit down in a nearby chair. Bob and Andy were still right by my side.

I slipped my lucky tee back into my pocket. I knew I would need it at least one more time as we went back down the mountain. I gathered my thoughts and tried to bring my breathing back under control.

Our group had time to explore before the other groups arrived and activities began. We were going to hike, eat, watch a movie on the history of the tram and spend time exploring the top of the mountain.

"Colt, let's go," I heard a girl call out across the hall. I turned to see Mandy and the rest of our group moving toward a huge staircase.

"You got this; you'll be fine. We'll still be here when it's time to go back down," said Andy.

"Try to enjoy the view," Bob added.

"I'll be right there," I said as I motioned toward the bathroom. I went inside and splashed some cold water on my face. The color was starting to return. *I have survived half of my nightmare.*

I walked out and joined my assigned group. Our first stop was the scenic overlook.

As we neared the top of the stairs, we turned and took a left. We stepped outside, and I was amazed.

SNOW!

For the first time in my life, I was seeing real snow! Kids were sticking out their tongues to catch the falling snowflakes. When we had left the valley, the temperature was in the mid-70s; now it was only around 30°.

Seeing snow was amazing! The small white snowflakes floated lazily in the air before landing on the ground. If Bob and Andy were here, we'd definitely have an epic snowball fight.

We took pictures, and I stayed far away from the edge of the lookout. Watching the lazy snowflakes falling helped settle my nerves even more.

The rest of the afternoon was filled with fun activities. Time flew by, and I was shocked when our guide told us it was time to meet back at the Mountain Station. I was having so much fun, I had almost forgotten that we still had to go back down to the bottom of the mountain.

As we gathered together, the teacher had us line up in our assigned groups to ride the tram. Apparently, they were sending us down earlier than originally planned. As the line dwindled, I kept looking over my shoulder for Bob and Andy. They were nowhere in sight.

Has their group already gone down? Or were they assigned to follow in a later group?

I wasn't sure what had happened. All I knew

was the time had come for our group to board the tram. We squeezed in, and I headed back to the middle railing.

Even though the car was full of people, I still felt alone.

-32-

The tram finally filled with no sign of Bob or Andy. They won't be able to save me this time. I watched in fright as the door closed. I put my head down as the tram jerked to life and started the descent back toward the Valley Station.

"Hey, Colt! Isn't this cool?" an excited voice whispered next to me. Marissa and Mandy both stood by me as the tram began its journey down the mountain.

I stood up a little taller and cleared my throat. "Yeah, super cool," I responded.

"I think so too," said Marissa.

I stood there smiling as the three of us talked about our day. I wasn't even paying attention as the operator came on over the loud speaker to announce the first transfer.

Suddenly the tram shook and swung back and forth. I was unprepared, and I couldn't control the involuntary little scream.

"You're so funny, Colt," giggled Mandy.

"The first transfer is done," said Marissa.

I smiled and looked toward them. In the background, I could see the mountains. My knees started to shake, but I tried my best to stop them before the girls noticed.

I was doing a good job of faking my way down the mountain. I put my right hand in my pocket and clutched my lucky tee while taking some deep breaths.

Minutes later we passed two more transfers, leaving only two more to survive. I tried not to look as I remembered how high both of the first transfer stations were.

"So, tell me about this golf tournament you have coming up," Mandy asked.

"Last week, I qualified for the Best of the West,

and the tournament is this Saturday," I said. Mandy's eyes grew wide as she looked at me, and I could tell she was impressed.

"Can you do me a huge favor?" Marissa asked.

"Sure, I guess. What can I do?" I asked her.

"Can you get me Brady Matthew's autograph?" Marissa sweetly begged.

"Well, I can see," I said.

She smiled.

I wanted his autograph too, but I thought that would be kind of pathetic since I was competing against him.

The girls continued to talk to me, and I enjoyed being the center of attention.

In fact, I was enjoying it too much.

The good news was that I had temporarily forgotten that we were moving down a huge mountain in a tram car held up by one small cable. The bad news was that I wasn't paying attention to the operator and wasn't prepared as we hit the next transfer tower.

I was halfway through a sentence when the car

jerked and dipped. I had my hand in my pocket, and I was holding my lucky tee. When I pulled my hand from my pocket to grip the railing, the tee came out too, I watched in horror as my lucky tee went flying. It landed, rolled, and went underneath the side of the tram. As I watched it fall thousands of feet to the valley below, I felt tears pricking my eyes.

My lucky tee is gone.

The operator turned up the music and blasted, "My Girl" by the Temptations. The entire group started to sing along as the music filled the car. Everyone but me seemed to be having the time of their lives.

My problems just seemed to be getting worse and worse. The tournament was two days away, and Pro's tee—the one that meant so much to both of us—was gone.

I was about to play in one of the biggest junior golf tournaments in the world against the best competition—without my good luck charm.

The tee was gone forever.

I can't seem to catch a break. Sure, I had survived and actually enjoyed the ride down the tram much more than the ride up.

But now my lack of confidence would be center stage at the Best of the West. I would be going into the tournament without Pro's lucky tee.

-33-

My legs felt like jelly as we exited the tram, and my feet were back on the ground at Valley Station. The field trip went much better than I could have hoped, but if I never have to ride the tram again, I would be perfectly fine!

As we walked toward our bus in Lot F, I could see that most of the students were already waiting for us.

Bob and Andy ran up.

"Colt, you did it!" Bob said, giving me a high five.

"I did it, and I'm still alive," I said with a shaky grin.

"He loved it," Marissa said as she walked past.

"Yeah, right," I said once she was out of earshot.

"You good?" Andy asked.

"Yeah. Taking that ride was rough, but I'm all right," I said.

We boarded the bus and rode back to school. Mom was waiting to take me to Mountain Valley for a 3:30 p.m. tee time with Pro. We only had two days left to practice for the tournament.

"Did you have fun?" Mom asked as I opened the passenger door.

"Fun? I wouldn't exactly call riding the tram fun," I replied. "But let's just say I didn't pass out this time. I actually made it to the top, and the ride was interesting. Still, I'm so glad it's over. I can't believe some people do that for fun!"

Mom drove at a brisk pace, knowing that Pro would be waiting for me and ready to practice.

"Colt, I'm so proud of you!"

"Thanks, Mom, but I'd rather not talk about it!"

"Oh no, Honey, I wasn't talking about the tram. I was talking about this," she said, handing me a folded copy of a newspaper.

As soon as I opened the sports page, the headline flashed in large block letters: ***BRADY MATTHEW ARRIVES IN PALM SPRINGS.***

Beneath a giant, color photo of Brady Matthew was an article about the Best of the West.

Confused, I turned to look at my mom.

"Turn to page B-6," she said with excitement.

I quickly flipped toward the back of the sports section before finding B-6. I scanned the text and toward the end of the paragraph, I read,

> Local La Quinta native, Colt Taylor, qualified last week at the Trilogy, making him eligible for this weekend's tournament.

While having my name mentioned in the sports section was pretty neat, a part of me was jealous of Brady. The young golfing prodigy had a front-page picture and an entire article written about him. Yet, here in my own hometown, my name was hard to find.

The newspaper article confirmed one thing: Brady-Matthew-mania was going to take over

PGA West's Best of the West Junior Golf Tournament, and I had a front-row seat. As we pulled into the golf course, I spotted Pro hitting balls at the driving range.

His long and lean silhouette filled the skyline with every perfect swing.

I hustled over to him, my conscience filled with guilt over losing his lucky tee.

"Colt," he greeted with a confident nod.

I started my warm-up routine that Pro had taught me. I started hitting with my wedges, then moved to my irons, before finally hitting my woods and driver.

I was stiff and tense, and my swing wasn't smooth. The tension and stress from the tram ride were still causing problems for me.

Pro could tell. "Colt, let's take a short break," he suggested.

"Okay," I said as I walked back to my golf bag.

"Is everything all right?" Pro asked. "I know you have a lot going on this weekend."

"I've had a long day," I said.

The Last Green

"Is that all?" Pro asked, sensing I wasn't telling the whole story.

With the Best of the West kicking off Saturday morning, I knew I didn't have time to waste.

Turning toward the mountains so I didn't have to make eye contact, I said, "I lost the tee. Today, I lost the special tee you gave me."

"The tee? Really?" Pro questioned in a low, shocked voice. I was trying to read his body language to see how disappointed he was, but I couldn't tell. Instead, he turned and walked back toward his golf bag. I saw him unzip a small side pocket and walk back toward me.

"Here," he said, handing me a handful of new tees. All of the golf tees looked exactly like the special one he had given me before.

"What's this?" I asked.

"Well, it's a bunch of special tees," he said with a smile.

Obviously, my "lucky" tee was only one of a normal one out of Pro's golf bag—like the others he held in his hand.

Confused, I looked back at him.

"Colt, it was never about the golf tee; it was about *you!* A tee or a charm doesn't make you lucky; you simply believed it would work, so it did," he explained.

At first, I felt cheated. All this time I had thought something was special or unique about the golf tee Pro had given me.

The golf tee wasn't special; *I was*. I just needed to believe it.

-34-

On Friday, the entire school was filled with excitement. Most eighth graders already looked at Friday as the best day of the week because it meant the weekend was almost here.

The cafeteria was also serving their famous Friday chocolate chip cookies—giant, moist, and loaded with chocolate chips—for a dollar. One boy, Jimmy Smith, once bought five of them and ate them all before leaving our lunch table! Jimmy now held the school record.

When I walked in the lunchroom, I wasn't surprised by how loud and electric the atmosphere was. A special, unusual energy seemed to be permeating the entire school.

I bought two of the supersized cookies and located Bob and Andy already eating at our usual table. Neither had touched their lunch but they were both mowing down one of the huge chocolate chip cookies.

"Tomorrow's a big day," Bob said between giant bites.

"Yeah, I'm kind of ready to get it over with," I said, trying to sound chill.

"Man, you need to enjoy this opportunity. You get to play at PGA West. You're going to be walking the same fairways that so many PGA legends have played," said Andy.

"Hey, Colt," called a girl as she walked by our table.

"Dude, she's an eighth grader," Bob said in awe.

"Yeah, weird. I don't know who she is," I said.

"But she knows you; everyone knows you by now," said Andy with a proud smile.

Several other students waved or said something to me as they walked by our table.

"What's going on?" I asked.

"Haven't you seen the paper?" asked Andy.

"Yeah, my mom showed me yesterday. It wasn't a big deal though; my name was barely even mentioned," I answered.

"No, I'm talking about *today's* paper," said Andy as he pulled a newspaper from his back pocket.

He opened it to the sports section. The headline was about spring baseball, but below was a picture of me from last week's tournament. The small photo tag read, *Is local golfing phenom Colt Taylor ready for big-time competition?*

I felt my face heat up. I was happier with yesterday's small recognition; this comment made me feel uncomfortable.

"Enjoy it! You're going to be a legend around here," exclaimed Andy.

"I'd do anything to be on the front page of the sports section," said Bob wistfully.

When I had qualified for the Best of the West, I guess that I wasn't aware of the attention that would come my way before the tournament.

All I wanted to do was golf. I didn't need any of

the attention that came with it. Let Brady have all the front-page articles and fame.

I just want to golf.

I knew that with attention came pressure. Not only was I playing for myself and Pro, but now all of the Coachella Valley.

The Best of the West brought the best junior golfers from all over the world.

Do I really belong in that group?

The last thing I wanted to do was embarrass everyone from La Quinta.

The newspaper article only added to an already too big spotlight. I was much happier when the spotlight was shining only on Brady; I just wanted to avoid the light pointed in my direction.

But I couldn't. The entire valley knew I was competing in the tournament tomorrow.

Suddenly, I lost my appetite. Even the enormous chocolate chip cookie in front of me no longer looked appetizing.

If I shanked a shot or missed an easy putt, everyone would know. Everyone would be following my every move. I closed my eyes and could see the crowd watching, staring, and judging.

All my friends and schoolmates would be paying attention to the tournament. The crowd of onlookers was growing larger and larger by the second.

My classmates were excited for me, but my anxiety was starting to lead to more and more negative thoughts. I wanted to be excited about this awesome opportunity, but I was so nervous.

What if I play horrible tomorrow? Can I even swing successfully with the whole world watching?

The thoughts of the golf tournament were starting to eat away at my insides. I felt like I was going to throw up.

I was relieved when the lunch bell finally rang, signaling us to return to class.

The excitement that I had for the tournament was slowly starting to get lost in all my fear.

Complete panic was starting to set in.

Am I even good enough to be there?

Should I even be attempting this?

-35-

Our last practice that night went well. We played some of the smaller par-3 holes at Mountain Valley, focusing on my short game.

Pro watched sharply as I hit my irons and chipped. I had learned so much from him on how to hit good precision putts. We spent the last hour studying the various slopes and breaks on the green.

"You're ready, Colt," said Pro.

"I'm not sure. It's so much easier to do it when it's just us," I said.

"Then it should be easy to do tomorrow. Golf is the most mental sport you will ever play. The best golfers block out everything and just see their next shot," said Pro.

The Last Green

Pressure to perform in front of people is nothing new when it comes to playing sports. Big games and large crowds seem to affect people differently. Sometimes athletes have their best games in front of people because of the adrenaline rush and excitement of performing for them.

Golf is a completely different sport. Staying calm and avoiding high rushes of adrenaline is important when golfing.

That night I tossed and turned in bed.

Good and bad golf shots kept replaying in my mind. I felt that if I stayed focused, I could golf with the best. However, I also knew that if I let the crowds of spectators get in my head, the day could easily become frustrating.

One hundred thirty-two golfers had qualified from all over the world, and they were likely having the same thoughts as I was. Well, maybe 131 of them were; I didn't imagine Brady Matthew was too nervous.

I fell asleep to visions of Pro's talking me through my swing.

The next morning, I was up before my alarm clock. I usually had trouble getting a restful night of sleep before a tournament. I also had a fear of my alarm not going off and missing everything. I always set three alarms on my phone and had my parents set one too.

I showered and dressed. I ate a small breakfast consisting of half a bagel and a glass of orange juice, but even this small fare was hard to get down today. I always ate a light breakfast when I was golfing.

My official tee time was 9:28 a.m. I wanted to be on the course by 7:30 a.m., so I had enough time to hit some range balls and putt. We pulled into PGA West a little after seven o'clock.

I got out and headed toward the range. Pro was already there, pacing as I headed in his direction.

The first day of the tournament would be played at the PGA West Pete Dye Mountain Course. The course, which is tucked into the base of the Santa Rosa Mountains, features elevated tee boxes and bunkered greens. The challenging course also provides golfers gorgeous views of the surrounding mountains. Being able to play the Pete Dye course is incredible. Many golfers include this course on their bucket list of the ones they wished to play someday.

My muscles were tight as I walked toward Pro. I noticed the course was already starting to fill up with staff and players.

Having never played in a PGA Junior National tournament, I was amazed at all the activity.

When I got to the driving range, I stretched and warmed up with my pitching wedge.

Pro approached me.

"Good morning, Colt. What a great day for golf!" he said.

I smiled because I knew that's why so many people travel to our area. Every day is a great day to golf in beautiful Palm Springs.

"It sure is," I agreed.

"The game of golf is simple; we're the ones who want to make it complicated. Remember *straight* is good; simply focus on keeping the ball straight," said Pro.

I had golfed hundreds of times on many courses, but today felt different.

Another unique aspect about the Best of the West tournament was each golfer had to use a caddy. That meant our coaches could be on the course with us at all times.

I was thrilled because that meant that Pro and I could talk before every shot. That small simple change helped lower my stress level. I knew I wouldn't be alone on the course; I'd have Pro.

I was just wrapping up my warm-ups when I heard a noise coming from the clubhouse located directly behind us. I turned to see a large group of people, flashing cameras, and journalists surrounding someone.

"Remember, Colt, you're not playing against Brady Matthew. Every time you golf, you're playing against yourself," Pro advised.

-36-

On the first day of the tournament, I shared a foursome with two kids from the East Coast and one from Texas.

Brady was teeing off at 11:00 a.m., so the tee box on hole #1 was pretty quiet when we started at 9:28 a.m. I was second off the tee. The guy before me had hit a solid drive down the fairway. I went through my pre-shot routine and blasted my drive. The ball hit in the fairway, rolling off into the longer grass. Mine wasn't a bad start, but I knew I'd have to be in the fairway most of the day if I wanted to compete in this tournament.

I parred the hole, along with two other golfers in our group. The fourth one shot a bogey.

I took a deep breath to steady my nerves as we walked up to the tee box on hole #2. The second hole was one of the hardest on the course—a short par 3 with water hazards down the left fairway. I played my tee shot to the right of the hole and had an easy chip onto the green. I made my short putt while everyone else bogeyed the hole.

We played the front nine at a good pace, and I was gaining confidence with each hole. Once I knew that I could actually compete with these guys, I started to play better. My confidence was growing on every hole, and I really started to get hot toward the end of the front nine, shooting back-to-back birdies on #8 and #9.

We finished the front nine, and I was four under par. I was two shots better than one of the guys and five shots better than the other two.

I didn't get too excited, and neither did Pro.

On the back nine, I kept getting better. I started off with a birdie on the par 4 tenth hole and a par on #11, another par four. My chip off the fringe on #11 almost went in, which was exciting.

The Last Green

Hole #14 is where I started to make a strong push. I blasted a drive down the right side of the fairway narrowly avoiding a huge sand bunker.

My second shot would be tough, and I struggled knowing what club to hit.

"Hit your seven here," Pro advised.

"I was thinking I'd use my eight iron from here," I said, feeling unsure.

"This shot is uphill. If you want to hit this elevated green, you must go up a club," explained Pro.

Good thing I listened to Pro! I hit my 7 iron and stuck it a couple of feet away from the flag. The other golfers in my group all hit the wrong club and had to chip to get on. My putt was still difficult, but after all that practice on the putting green with Pro, I was able to sink it for another birdie.

Now I was sitting at six under, and my confidence was soaring.

I parred both #15 and #16, but I bogeyed #17 when I missed an easy five-foot putt. Hole #18 was a long par five with a dogleg left. The hole is pretty intimidating from the tee box, having out of bounds on both sides. I looked down the left side that was filled with homes. On my right was the driving range which was clearly labeled out of bounds.

Straight, I thought to myself.

I reached for my driver.

"Hit your three wood here; straight is more important than a couple of extra yards," said Pro.

I slipped my driver back into my bag and clubbed down to my three wood. I hit a nice straight shot down the right side of the fairway, but I lost about 20 yards off my drive. I approached my ball and noticed it had a great, clean lie.

"Hit your three wood again; go for the green," said Pro.

This time I hesitated. In my mind, I was going to hit a nice #4 iron, putting myself about 100 yards from the green. I wasn't going to try to put it in with my second shot.

"Trust me, Colt. Hit your three wood. Swing it just like you hit it off the tee," he told me.

If I knew anything, I knew to trust Pro.

The Last Green

I grabbed my three wood and hit the ball. I watched as it bounced out of sight.

As I walked up to the green, I was shocked at the slope I couldn't see from the fairway, but Pro could tell. The flag was at the back of the green, and my ball had rolled right toward it. I had about an eight-foot putt for eagle.

The other players all had to chip on and had long putts. I had plenty of time to watch as they putted all over the green. It was almost 1:00 p.m., so I knew the greens would be much drier and faster than they had been this morning.

I put my ball two inches outside the right edge of the cup. I drew back one smooth straight putt and watched as the ball dropped into the cup.

I heard a small round of clapping and saw head nods from the other players.

I walked into the clubhouse happy that I had played so well. I was seven under par and had played one of my personal best rounds. I was shocked when I looked up at the leaderboard.

-37-

The leaderboard consisted of a bunch of names I didn't recognize.

As I scanned from the bottom up, I couldn't find my name. My eyes moved from the first page of scores onto the second.

"Well, would you look at that," Pro whispered.

At the top of the scoreboard, I recognized two names. Brady was in first place leading with a -10 under par, a new junior club record on the course.

I was tied in fourth place, with a -7 under par, read *Colt Taylor* in big, bold letters.

Not only was I in the top ten, but I was also in the top five! I walked back toward my golf bag in astonishment.

The Last Green

As I was working my way through the crowd, I heard an unfamiliar voice. "Hey, nice round," said the voice from behind me.

I turned to see Brady Matthew standing by a crowd of media people.

"Thank you," I managed to stutter, totally caught off guard. As I walked away, I heard Brady speak again. "Hey, Pro, hope all is well," he said.

As I kept walking, I was impressed that even the great Brady Matthew knew who Pro was. But then again, I figured everyone knew him. After all, he was a famous golfer.

"Man, even Brady knows you, Pro! That's cool," I said.

"Yep," Pro said quietly, as he kept moving along.

I stopped. I noticed something was off right away. "Do you know him?" I questioned.

Pro stopped and looked me in the eyes. "No, I don't know him…well, not anymore." He sighed before continuing. "Colt, before moving here to Palm Springs, I lived in Las Vegas. I used to work with Brady when he was younger. I gave him lessons when he first started golfing, but I haven't spoken to him in four years."

What? After all this time, Pro forgot to mention that he had worked with Brady Matthew?

I remembered then when I first saw him at the Mountain Valley that Tony had told me he had a bad experience instructing someone. "Why didn't you tell me about working with Brady?" I asked.

"Would that have helped improve your game?" he asked. "I didn't want to add any more distractions for you nor add more pressure on you. I worked with Brady at a very early age. He moved on to a different coach. There really isn't much to talk about," Pro stated and then walked away.

A representative of the *Palm Springs Daily Sun* called me over to interview me about the tremendous first day of the tournament. I had never been interviewed before, and I wasn't used to getting all this attention.

As the newspaper reporter was interviewing me, the sports broadcaster from Channel 5 stood in the background, waiting for me to finish.

"How do you feel about getting paired with Brady Matthew?" he asked.

Paired with Brady? This is news to me.

"Well, I haven't had a lot of time to think about it. I know I played good golf today, but I was still a little surprised to see my name on the leaderboard," I said humbly.

"Do you feel any added pressure knowing that your coach was his former coach?" the reporter pressured.

"No, I don't think so. I've learned a ton from Pro. I'm just thankful he moved to Palm Springs," I said with a smile.

The bright lights from the television camera were shining directly into my eyes, making me squint.

"One last question: do you feel any added pressure being a hometown underdog in such a huge tournament?" he asked.

"Pressure? I guess a little, but I know I need to keep the ball straight. Even a bad shot had better be straight," I answered.

The crowd laughed, but I wasn't trying to be funny. The most important lesson Pro had taught me was that a straight ball was the best kind of ball.

"Do you think you actually have a chance to win?" the reporter asked as I was walking away.

"Why not?" I said with a smirk.

-38-

As Dad and I pulled back into the house, Bob and Andy were sitting in their usual spot on our front porch.

They sprinted up to the car, excited.

"Colt, you played amazing!" said Bob.

"Fantastic job, my friend!" yelled Andy.

We went into the house. Mom had grilled some burgers and had made some French fries in the oven for all of us to eat.

"Quick, grab your plate, Colt! You're about to be a television star," Dad said, calling us to come into the living room. Channel Five was on the television, and the sports feature was about to come on.

"We have a special story unfolding at PGA West this weekend. The Best of the West PGA Junior Golf Tournament has invaded the valley," announced the sports reporter.

The camera cut to different scenes from today's action on the golf course.

"Like something out of a movie, a better showdown couldn't have been planned for the finals tomorrow. We have superstar Brady Matthew taking on the entire field of challengers. Even though Brady is the clear favorite, one golfer will have an obvious advantage," he said.

The television then panned to a different reporter—the same one I had talked to outside the PGA Clubhouse.

"That's right! What a day tomorrow will be! We have the young superstar versus his former teacher," he said.

Dad cocked his head toward me. "What's he talking about, Colt?" Dad asked.

"I guess Pro used to work with Brady when he was younger or something," I mumbled.

The Last Green

Dad nodded like it was no big deal.

"When we asked Colt if he thought Brady was as good as advertised, Colt gave us a different answer than we expected. He wasn't afraid to throw a little shade toward Brady," said the reporter with a twinkle in his eye.

"No, I don't think so. I've learned a ton from Pro. I'm just thankful he moved to Palm Springs."

Dad quickly turned and glared at me. "Colt!" he boomed.

"Dad, he changed his words and the context! The question he asked me was if I felt any added pressure knowing Pro had coached Brady," I said defensively.

Too late I knew our local news broadcast hadn't done anything to help me; in fact, they had only made it worse. I was in complete shock and disbelief. I couldn't believe how the video had been so skillfully edited.

Seemingly as soon as I did something good, something bad happened. Flying under the radar would now be impossible. Attention was the last thing I wanted; all I cared about was focusing and playing good golf.

We sat quietly in the living room before Bob finally spoke up.

"Well, I'm glad I got a ticket for tomorrow. I just know something crazy is going to happen," he said.

-39-

I woke up and wiped the sleep from my eyes after another night of restless sleep.

I got dressed and headed out to the kitchen. Dad was already up, making scrambled eggs, toast, and bacon. I knew Dad was excited, and I wondered if he had even slept.

I sat down as he put some food on my plate. I didn't have much of an appetite, but I knew I had to have something in my stomach for the morning round of golf.

"Dad, why would that news guy do that? I never said it like that," I said, still puzzled.

"Son, sometimes in life people will twist the situation to make their story better. I know you would never say that, and Pro knows you would never say it too," he said.

"What about Brady?" I asked.

"Kids like Brady deal with this kind of nonsense all the time. Who knows if he even watched our local news last night." Dad shrugged.

Hearing that possibility made me feel a little better. I finished my plate and headed out to the garage. We drove to PGA West in silence as both of us thought about today's golf match.

The course was already busy and full of people when we pulled in.

I took my clubs to the driving range and started hitting some golf balls. Pro worked his way through the crowd toward me.

"Good morning, Colt. It's a good day for golf," he said with a nod.

"Yes, sir," I answered, waiting for Pro to say something about the news show.

I wanted to get ahead of the issue and tell Pro the truth.

"Pro, that news guy did me wrong. That's not

what I said. I mean I said it, but that was my answer to a different question he asked," I said.

With a look of pure confidence and focus, Pro said, "That's what they do. You have to block it all out now and forget all about that clip. I have something I want to show you."

He reached into his pocket and pulled out a small plastic bag.

"These last couple of weeks have been good for both of us, Colt. The first time I saw you swing, I knew you had something special. But you were missing one important element."

My mind flashed back to when both of us stood staring at our own reflection in the mirror at the pro shop.

Holding up the small plastic sandwich bag, Pro asked, "You see this?"

"Well, I see a plastic bag," I answered.

"No, you need to look much closer, Colt."

I squinted until I could finally see what appeared to be a number of very small seeds.

"My life changed years ago when I learned about

the power of a small mustard seed," explained Pro. "I read a book that changed my life forever, and I still read it every day. Among many other lessons, that book says if you have faith the size of a mustard seed, you can move a mountain."

As small as that mustard seed was, it seemed bigger than the confidence I had in myself before I met Pro. I realized that faith was the ingredient I had been missing in my golf game. Pro had his faith restored, and now he was trying to teach me to believe in myself.

"Look over there," Pro said, pointing to the Santa Rosa Mountain range that bordered the golf course.

His message was clear; today I had to choose faith over fear. My fear of failure, of large crowds, and of feeling that I wasn't good enough had stolen my self-faith. I needed it—even if it was only the size of a mustard seed.

I finally understood exactly what Pro had been trying to teach me.

I nodded in agreement.

The Last Green

A crowd of people had assembled on the practice tee next to me. I turned to see cameras and PGA West officials surrounding Brady.

He started hitting golf balls. I stood watching, admiring his swing. Everything was one smooth, connected motion.

He noticed me looking at him and stopped.

"Hey, sorry I didn't impress you much yesterday. I'll try to do better at that today," he said with a cocky smirk.

"Um, that's not what I meant. The reporter…"

Brady didn't give me a chance to explain what had happened as he walked away.

I guess Brady watches the local news after all.

-40-

Since we were the top-ranked group, a large crowd of followers were waiting for us on the first tee box. I wanted to say something to Brady but didn't know what to say. He had seen the sports piece, and I was sure he felt disrespected. I couldn't blame him either.

On most days, I knew he was way out of my league. But today wasn't most days.

The Pete Dye Stadium Course at PGA West is one of the best golf courses in the world. How fitting that the championship round was being played here! The course had been designed for high-level golf.

Brady was the first one on the tee box. He blasted his driver straight down the fairway. The first hole was a 358-yard par four. The other two golfers hit nice drives but not nearly as far as Brady.

It was my turn.

I took a deep breath and looked up at the mountain range. Today was a mountain-moving day.

"Faith the size of a mustard seed," I said to myself as I slowly exhaled and approached the ball.

I narrowed my focus and pulled back. My driver made great contact with the golf ball as the tee exploded breaking into pieces. My golf ball rocketed down the fairway, bounced and rolled past Brady's ball.

"Nice shot," he said, turning toward me.

I wiped my sweaty hands against my pant legs.

I had managed to hit a great shot and block out the people around me.

I couldn't have asked for a better start.

Our entire group parred the first hole. Everyone in this group was a really good golfer. Brady had missed a 15-foot putt for a birdie. The rest of us had longer putts but were able to lag them close for our second putt.

Throughout the next eight holes, Brady and I played incredible golf. I couldn't believe how well I was playing. These golfers were great, but their exceptional skill level simply pushed me to play even better.

After we finished the first nine holes, Brady held a two stroke lead; he was -9 under par. I was in second place, shooting -7. The other golfers were -5 under par.

"If I can keep this pace, I'll get second place," I told myself as we prepared to tee off on the 10th hole.

We grabbed a quick drink at the turn before heading to hole #10. Pro could sense something about me; maybe he saw a level of resignation on my face.

"You're playing great golf, but didn't you come here to win?" asked Pro, sensing I was content with second.

Win?

Pro didn't really think I could win, did he?

I was only two strokes back, which wasn't very

much. Brady left no room for mistakes or breakdowns. I simply had to keep my golf ball straight and in play.

"Faith the size of a mustard seed," I whispered before every tee shot.

On hole #11 and #12 I pushed Brady, and we both birdied each hole. By now, both of the other golfers had all but given up the hope of trying to beat us.

On #16 I hit an amazing chip from about 60 yards out that almost landed me a birdie. I finished the hole with a par.

Brady bogeyed, his only one on the back nine.

I was down one stroke as we approached one of the most dangerous golf holes imaginable. Hole #17 was designed to destroy a professional golfer's confidence.

What will it do to mine?

"You need to own #17," Pro said after I handed him my putter.

Here is where I will make my move on Brady. With only two holes left, it was now or never.

-41-

So far, I had stayed pretty composed and calm. Being here, just one stroke behind the lead, my confidence had totally shifted.

By now, I didn't just think I belonged there…I knew it! I also knew that when I was playing confident golf, I could hang with the best of the best.

I was flying high, ready to take on the next challenge, until we crested the hill and started walking toward Alcatraz.

The 166-yard par 3 is an island green like no other. Hitting the green is the only option because hitting anywhere else is a complete disaster. The green is completely surrounded by water and jagged rocks.

The Last Green

The crowd had been gaining in size as we came closer to the end of the championship round. The close match was bringing more attention to an already tense situation.

Since I had parred the last hole, I was on the tee box first, down a stroke to Brady. With only two holes remaining, I knew my time to be aggressive had come.

My knees started to shake as I teed up my golf ball. A week ago, I wouldn't have been able to hit this shot. I knew I could do it, but doubt was slowly starting to creep back into my mind as I looked toward that rocky island.

I grabbed my #5 iron. The wind was low, and I thought that if I hit it solidly, it would land safely at the back of the green.

"I think you should go with the #6," Pro said.

"I don't want to be short, though," I said.

"I get that, but you don't want to be long either," Pro said with a grin.

The green was so small, giving little room for any error.

Walking back to my golf bag, I dropped my #5 iron back and pulled out my #6 iron.

As I walked away, I turned to look at Pro one more time before lining up my ball. He had a confident look; his eyes were locked on the green.

I stood in the tee box and looked down toward the green. The large crowd grew silent as I readied my shot. I took a practice swing and backed off my ball one last time.

"Keep it straight. Faith the size of a mustard seed can move mountains," I repeated to myself. Pro had drilled these sayings into my mind. Even when we played Mountain Valley, Pro had been preparing me for this exact situation. His emphasis on hitting it straight was made for this very hole.

My vision tightened as I tried to block out all the dangers around me for this critical shot. Suddenly, the light-blue water and jagged rocks blurred, and I had tunnel vision toward the small green.

The whole sequence was strange. I felt like I was watching it all happen from above my body. I felt

The Last Green

like I was moving in slow motion as I drew back my club and swung.

The ball sailed straight toward the pin but was dropping fast.

Had I hit it hard enough? Did I use the wrong club? As the ball dropped, it looked as if it was going to splash into the water in front of the green.

The crowd started cheering and yelling.

I heard one man yell, "Go! GO!"

The ball hit with a loud thud as it landed directly on the other side of the rock face. The ball took a big bounce before landing in the middle of the green. The momentum carried the ball a little farther, setting up a ten-foot putt for a birdie.

The crowd erupted.

"Nice shot," Brady complimented as he approached the tee box.

I walked back to stand by Pro.

"You did it, Colt! You nailed it!" Pro exclaimed.

Brady took a practice swing, lined up his ball, and his iron shot toward the flag. The ball hit the back of the green and rolled back toward the hole.

He had landed it, but his putt was much farther away than mine.

The next two golfers hit into the water and had to take a penalty stroke. They had to hit their next shot from the predetermined drop zone, near the front of the water.

Walking toward the small land bridge that connected the green, I knew this was my chance to tie the match. I watched as the two other golfers chipped on from the drop zone, landing their ball on the green.

Once I walked onto the green, I was amazed at how small it was. *I can't believe I even hit it!* I marked my golf ball and strode toward Pro.

"It's going to break left, hard left. I would go two cups to the right," said Pro.

Puzzled, I went back and examined the putt.

"Are you sure?" I asked, unconvinced.

"I can see it near the cup; it's going to come back to the left," said Pro.

I lined up my putt, leading it two cup lengths outside the cup, and hit it.

The Last Green

The putt turned and looked like it was going way right but slowly started turning back to the left as it slowed near the hole.

Right before the hole, the ball rolled one more time before dropping into the cup.

Birdie!

Brady lined up his putt and missed it, but it was close enough for him to walk up and tap it in.

The match was tied.

I had one more hole, which meant one more chance to pull off the upset win over Brady.

Walking toward the 18th hole, I knew the tournament was going to come down to one shot.

All I had to do was win the last green, and I would beat Brady and be a champion!

-42-

The crowd on the 18th hole at PGA West was bigger than anything I had ever seen. The crowd on the 17th I had thought was huge was nothing compared to right now. Even the balcony at the clubhouse was full of onlookers.

I had proven to myself that I could golf with the best in the world. I finally saw what my dad and Pro saw when they watched me; I finally believed in myself.

My mustard-seed-size faith in myself had grown. I had to finish the game strong.

I had to win this last hole.

As we walked toward the 18th hole, I focused on hitting the fairway. This hole had destroyed many

The Last Green

a golfer's dreams. This long par 4 requires an excellent tee shot over a large pond. The fairway doglegs left and is littered with sand traps down the right hand side. I wasn't worried about the sand; I knew I only had to clear the pond.

After hitting a great shot on #17, the pond didn't look so intimidating.

Since I had the lowest score on Alcatraz, I was the first to tee it up.

My focus was sharp as I stared down the shot.

I looked over my right shoulder at the huge crowd that had gathered around the tee box. As I scanned the crowd, I saw a lot of unfamiliar faces. But the two I saw inspired me. Standing with giant grins of pride were Bob and Andy. My two best friends had followed me on the back nine and had a front-row seat on the 18th. I know they believed in me and my ability this whole time. Somehow, they had known I would be in this position and that I could win. They had faith in me.

"The last hole…just win the last hole," I kept telling myself.

Pro had been training me for this moment. I was thankful for both his skill in training and our mental preparation. All of his carefully taught lessons were coming into play on this last hole.

As I approached my bag, I reached for my driver.

Just as Pro was about to say something, I dropped my driver and grabbed my 3-wood. I knew he was going to tell me to hit the 3-wood, and that straighter was better than distance especially on the 18th.

I didn't need to hit a bomb, but if I didn't hit it straight, I'd be in big trouble.

I stepped up and hit a perfectly straight ball that landed and bounced twice in the fairway. The crowd cheered. I knew Brady would drive far past my ball, but it didn't bother me. My second shot had put me in a spot for a birdie putt.

Brady's drive roared off the tee and landed 40 yards in front of mine on the fairway. Two weeks ago, if someone would have told me that winning the Best of the West championship would come down to Brady and me, I would have thought they were crazy.

Other people had believed I could compete with him, but I hadn't.

Simply competing with him wasn't the case anymore; I knew I could win this hole. My second shot would be the one to help me win this tournament.

I looked to my right and saw danger. Sand traps littered the right side of my shot. One small mistake and I would be in the sand.

My left was even more dangerous; the pond covered the entire left side of the fairway and ran past the hole.

This shot had to be straight, which wasn't a problem.

I laughed to myself. I confidently grabbed my 5-iron from my bag. I looked at Pro, who was standing quietly. I knew he was pleased with my club choice.

My practice swings were perfect, and I could feel the balanced weight of the iron in my hand.

I stood over the ball, and the rest of the world went fuzzy. The gorgeous mountains, the water, and the sand traps disappeared as I zeroed in on the green, the very last green.

My swing was confident as I hit the golf ball perfectly. I watched as it hit on the fringe of the green, bounced twice and rolled on toward the flag.

I had an easy six-foot putt for birdie. I couldn't have hit a better shot.

The pressure was on Brady. If he didn't put his ball close, the tournament was mine!

I watched with intrigue as Brady approached his ball. It looked like he had grabbed an 8-iron. He was much closer than me and had a better shot to the green.

Without hesitation, he swung, rocketing his ball toward the green. His ball landed hard on the back of the green and slowly rolled down toward the pin, leaving him a 12-foot putt for birdie.

He had stuck his shot.

-43-

The other two players had to hit out of the drop zone because their second shots ended up in the water once again. They were starting to unravel on the last two holes. Once they chipped on, I approached the green.

My putt looked straight, and Pro thought so too. I had made this putt a thousand times.

Brady's putt was much harder than mine, as he had to go uphill.

The two other boys tapped in their putts, leaving only Brady and me on the green.

I could barely watch as he slowly lined up his putt. Brady was taking his time and talking it over with his caddy.

The huge crowd had followed us from the tee box to the green. We were completely surrounded by a sea of people.

Brady crouched down one last time to read his putt.

Then he picked up his ball marker and replaced it with his ball. He wasted no time and without overthinking it, reached back and putted. His stroke was pure, straight, and perfect. The ball rolled straight and fell into the cup. He had just made a difficult birdie putt, and the crowd roared.

What an amazing shot!

My heart sank. Now I had to make this putt to tie and force an extra hole playoff.

I stepped back and read the putt several times. I drew in a deep breath and stood over my ball.

Without another thought, I stood over my ball and pulled back my putter. I knew I was going to make this putt.

The face of the putter hit perfectly, and I watched as the ball rolled toward the hole. There was no break; it was a perfectly straight putt.

The Last Green

The ball started to slow down much faster than I had anticipated.

"Go! Go!" I muttered, wishing I would have put a little more power behind my putt.

The crowd hushed as the golf ball stopped on the outside edge of the cup.

I waited for it to drop in the hole. *It has to...*

But it didn't. The ball stopped just short of the hole.

I had left the putt short by less than an inch.

My dreams of beating the great Brady Matthew were left short.

I stood in disbelief.

I didn't know how to respond. My eyes started to well up, and I could tell I was about to lose it. I felt a hand on my back and turned.

"You played fantastic today! What a great round!" said Brady with his hand extended.

"Congratulations," I mustered.

"You have a bright future, I'll look you up the next time you come to the valley," he said with a genuine smile.

"That would be cool," I agreed.

He shook my hand and was off toward the clubhouse, followed by an entourage of fans and media personalities. I walked over to my ball.

How did this putt not go in?

As I looked down to tap in the ball, I stopped. The ball had literally sat just on the lip of the cup.

I couldn't believe my eyes as I dropped to my knees. The distance from the putt dropping in was so small. I could only see a small section of green, about the size of the mustard seed, between the ball and the outside edge of the cup.

I was short ... by a mustard seed.

After tapping in my putt, I walked toward Pro, who reached out and drew me to him with a big hug. "I am so proud of you, Colt. You did it!" he said proudly.

"No, I lost Pro. I *almos*t did it," I said.

"Colt, you will have hundreds of putts and chances to win golf tournaments. You took on the best in the world in front of all these people and played amazing golf," he said.

The Last Green

I was glad to hear Pro say he was proud of me.

The next thing I remember was being mobbed by Bob and Andy.

"You were amazing!" exclaimed Bob.

"Yeah, you were crushing the ball today, Colt," said Andy.

Walking toward the clubhouse, I knew that match hadn't come down to the last green or a missed putt.

I smiled. I didn't win the tournament, but I had won something much more important, self-confidence.

Golf Terms

Back nine: Holes 10-18 on an 18-hole course

Birdie: Completing the hole in one less stroke than the par (2 on a par 3)

Bogey: Completing the hole in one more stroke than the par (4 on a par 3)

Chip: a short, low shot near the green that usually lands on the green

Dogleg: A bend to the left or the right in fairways; a hole that isn't straight

Double bogey: Completing the hole in two more strokes than the par

Drive: Hitting the ball into play from the tee box

Eagle: Completing the hole in two fewer strokes than the par (1 on a par 3)

Fairway: The stretch of shorter grass that extends from the tee to the green that are cut short for the ball to roll

Fringe: The collar of higher mown grass that surrounds the green

Green: The area of shortest grass with a smooth surface where the hole is located

Hazards: Water, sand traps, and tall grass to make playing golf more challenging

Hole-in-One: Hitting the ball in the hole on your first shot

Irons: The metal clubs numbered to correspond with their lofts, each of which will hit the ball a certain height and distance

Out of Bounds: areas outside the golf course from which play is not allowed

Par: The expected number of strokes a golfer should take to get the ball in the hole

Putter: The flat-faced club that rolls the ball to the hole with as few putts as possible

Shank: probably the most destructive shot in golf; hitting the ball with the hosel of the club and sending it to the right at a 45° to 90° angle

Stroke: The forward movement of the club made to strie the ball

Tee: the peg that is pushed in the ground to set the ball on

Tee Box: The designated area that marks the beginning of each hole

Tee Time: The exact time that your round of golf starts

Wood: Golf clubs made with big round heads that go the farthest

About the Author

Lane Walker is an award-winning author, educator and highly sought-after speaker. Walker started his career as a fifth grade teacher before transitioning into educational administration, serving as a highly effective principal for over 12 years. He has coached football, basketball and softball.

Lane paid his way through college working as a news and sports reporter for a newspaper. He grew up in a hunting-and-fishing fanatical house, with his owning a taxidermy business.

After college, he combined his love for writing and the outdoors. For the past 20 years, he has been an outdoor writer, publishing over 250 articles in newspapers and magazines.

Walker's Hometown Hunters Collection won a Moonbeam Bronze Medal for Best Book Series Chapter Books. His second series, The Fishing Chronicles, won a Moonbeam Gold Medal for Best Book Series Chapter Books.

Lane launched a brand-new, sports-themed book collection called Local Legends in the spring of 2022.

Stay tuned! More exciting chapter books by Lane will be released in the future!

Visit:
www.bakkenbooks.com

Made in the USA
Coppell, TX
27 August 2024